Faith, Courage, and Wisdom

Faith, Courage, and Wisdom

A Journey to Manhood

Nevlynn L. Johnson, Sr.

Writers Club Press
New York Lincoln Shanghai

Faith, Courage, and Wisdom
A Journey to Manhood

Writers Club Press
an imprint of iUniverse, Inc.

For information address:
iUniverse
2021 Pine Lake Road, Suite 100
Lincoln, NE 68512
www.iuniverse.com

ISBN: 0-595-16741-1 (Pbk)
ISBN: 0-595-74570-9 (Cloth)

Printed in the United States of America

This book is dedicated to my son, Nevlynn L. Johnson II, the love of my life. Thanks for bringing me so much joy.
And
To my Dad, Kenneth Brown. Pops, your death was not in vain. You live through me and the grandson you were never able to see.

"…but we also rejoice in our sufferings, because we know that suffering produces perseverance; perseverance, character; and character, hope."
Romans 5:3-4

Acknowledgements

A work such as this takes a lot of personal commitment and collaboration to complete. There is no way that I would have reached this point without the special help of many people.

First and foremost, I give all glory to God for allowing me to be where I am today. I purely recognize that it has been God that has orchestrated my life, and I am humbled and in total gratitude to God for this.

Next would be my new bride, Meketa, and amazing new son, Leyton Meade. They have both been so wonderful as I have worked hard on the finishing touches of this book. Meketa was understanding and supportive on many nights when I had to shut myself off from the world to work on the book. She even pushed me to write and gave so many great suggestions to make this book better. Thanks sweetie, and thanks Leyton for cooing through many nights as I read.

My many friends have been so intricately involved in this process too. David Gushee has been a great friend and support not only during this book but at other times in my life. Thanks David.

Last but not least is my mom who was the first person to encourage me to write this book. A great teacher, she taught me to persevere. To her credit, she made something out of nothing. May God continue to bless and enrich your life forever. Thanks so much, Mom!

Contents

Acknowledgements vii

Introduction (*Dr. David Gushee*) xi

Preface xiii

Part One: Formation 1

    Chapter 1—Chaos 3

    Chapter 2—I Am Pregnant 9

    Chapter 3—Daddy 13

    Chapter 4—My Hero 23

    Chapter 5—Our New House 29

    Chapter 6—Tent Revival 37

Part Two: New World Order 41

    Chapter 7—The Big Move 43

    Chapter 8—Diversity 49

    Chapter 9—Deerpath 55

    Chapter 10—The Work Ethic 57

Part Three: Lone Star 63

    Chapter 11—Texas, Here We Come 65

    Chapter 12—Tubby 71

    Chapter 13—Westheimer 75

Part Four: Identity Crisis 85

 Chapter 14—Flint: The Return *87*

 Chapter 15—Throw down *93*

 Chapter 16—High School Love *99*

 Chapter 17—Russell Street *105*

 Chapter 18—Graduation *109*

Part Five: The Real World 115

 Chapter 19—Reality Check *117*

 Chapter 20—Brandy *125*

 Chapter 21—Looking for Love *131*

 Chapter 22—Harassment *139*

Part Six: Transformation 143

 Chapter 23—Persistence *145*

 Chapter 24—A New Faith *151*

 Chapter 25—Called *159*

 Chapter 26—Bluegrass Country *171*

 Chapter 27—Seminary *181*

 Chapter 28—Teen Life *187*

 Chapter 29—A NEW BIRTH *193*

 Chapter 30—Curve Ball *197*

 Chapter 31—Friends *203*

Epilogue: Finale 207

About the Author 219

Introduction

Most thirty-something men haven't lived long enough to even consider writing an autobiography. But most thirty-something men also haven't stood in the street while bullets whizzed by their head, or had their father and father-figure murdered, or survived the mean streets of Flint, Michigan, and the racist streets of Humble, Texas.

Nevlynn Johnson tells a compelling tale in the pages that follow. When he concludes that "realistically, there is no way I should be living," he is not exaggerating. His story is much like that of many of the urban poor of America: raised by a single mother, left by an absent and ne'er do well father, struggling to survive the drug, gun, and gang culture of the streets as well as our violent and wretched urban schools, and—when he makes it out of black urban America into the white promised land—he is confronted by the pervasive impact of both overt and subtle racism.

Yet Nevlynn's story takes a dramatic turn, for here is a survivor of those mean streets and of that racism. The author looks back on his story with a sense of awe and humble gratitude, for this endangered young man not only survived the streets but made it out. How this happened is of interest not only in itself but also to anyone who cares about economic empowerment and moral survival in urban America.

The clues are scattered throughout the story. They include the indispensable working mother, who despite all odds and her own immaturity, manages to pull her life together and to obtain a college education. Education opens the door out of Flint, and government aid, and the misery of poverty.

We also see clues in the formation of Nevlynn's own character. Discovering as a teenager that if he wants nice clothes and other goodies he will have to work for them, Nevlynn develops an indomitable work ethic. Realizing that the life of the street is a dead-end, he steers clear of it while also managing not to be destroyed by those who prey on weakness. His involvements with young women are presented here, but we see a strong sense of responsibility and self-control throughout the perilous dating years. His mental toughness carries him through the soul-testing process of induction into the military. In dealing with racism Nevlynn learns not to put up with it and how to interact successfully with a predominantly white world.

And then there is grace. In the most unlikely places Nevlynn experiences the transforming grace of God: an urban tent revival, a lily-white Anchorage Baptist church, and among white friends who carry him through the pain of his divorce. Here is a faith not for the comfortable but for the afflicted; a story of God's love in a broken and hateful world.

White Americans rarely choose to, or are permitted to enter into the world of urban black America in the way we have opportunity to do so in this book. It is a frightening world in many ways, and Nevlynn Johnson does not pretend that this world's pathologies are anything other than what they are. And yet struggling to survive, to redeem, and to leave these areas are millions of human beings, sacred human beings, made in God's image and worthy of a decent shot at life.

I am grateful to God that my friend Nevlynn Johnson made it out— only to reenter it in ministry. I can only pray that thousands upon thousands of others will do the same, and that suburban white Christian Americans will do all they can to work for the reclamation of every soul and every blighted city in America.

I hope that many thousands of readers will read this work and mark its lessons well.

Dr. David Gushee, Professor of Moral Philosophy
Union University
Jackson, Tennessee

Preface

In many ways this book reflects much of my new-found perspective on life, a perspective that was difficult for me to clearly understand prior to this point. As I wrote, each chapter became a renewal and rebirth for me. Though I struggled while reflecting on some of the darkest times of my life, I know that these reflections were extremely beneficial to my maturity as a Christian man. The culmination of them became a major contribution to my healing. All of who I was and who I am becoming is wrapped up in this work.

What I have put forth in this book for the reader is a realistic look at the evolution of a young black man living in a black sub-culture while surviving in mainstream white culture. My difficulties and challenges in the variety of roles, stereotypes, and responsibilities are heartfelt and expressed in the simplest ways possible. In other words, I did my best to keep it real. Besides that, my life experiences were real, and there is no need to inflate or deflate that reality.

This work depicts only one of the many diverse life experiences of black boys growing up amidst cultural and racial clashes in society. If my story gives hope to them, or to those who work with young boys and girls in the inner city or with kids going through extreme transitional points in their lives, then I will have accomplished one of my major tasks, for it is in this hope that many young people will find life. It only takes someone loving and being patient to make a difference in the life of another person. Many such people crossed my path, but God has been the absolute support for me. Neither my life experiences nor environment were the conclusive factors in determining my place in life.

As I have worked with teenagers and children at risk, I have seen volunteers and others from a variety of backgrounds give up hope for these kids. I see myself as one of "these" kids. We—and I include myself—have a knack for giving up on people whose lives appear to be going nowhere. I have a particular heart for children and teens who often have been told so many negative things about themselves and their situations.

I challenge whoever reads this book to go beyond giving up on people, particularly kids. For all practical purposes, people should have given up on me, but they didn't, and that made a tremendous difference. My family background, environment, and early teachings were not healthy; had I not been redirected, I would probably be dead. My life had all the markings of failure, yet somehow things turned just the opposite. Often, all it takes is for one person to believe in another. That belief is powerful, especially when everything around you dictates the complete opposite.

With all the negativity and angst in the world, it is surprising to me that any of us living in challenging situations make it out. This is where God steps in, which is not to say that He doesn't step into other, less stressful situations. I just have a sense that God enjoys loving and empowering the underdog.

There were times when my mother made a difference for sure. She was the one adult I could depend on for moral support. However, it is God's hand on my life that has enabled me to be where I am today. Without question, I was the poster boy for the underdog, and in some ways this may still be the case.

I can honestly say that my place on earth today is not the result of programs, people, or positive thinking. My place on earth today has come only by the will of God. Programs, people, and yes, an optimistic mindset got me through many a day, but those things are not and never have been the final authority of my destiny.

As a result, I can now graciously accept my position in life and enjoy where I am right now with the understanding that this certain place or station will not be my final stomping ground. My life is a journey of growing closer to God and investing in human relationships around me. My hope is that my finite existence will make a positive and significant difference in the life of someone else for the purposes of God's Kingdom. God has His hands on my life and yours. Allow Him to take you places where you aren't able to go by yourself. And remember, never give up, especially when it looks the darkest.

Be blessed!   *Nev*

"But we have this treasure in earthen vessels, that the surpassing greatness of the power may be of God and not from ourselves." 2 Corinthians 4:7

PART ONE

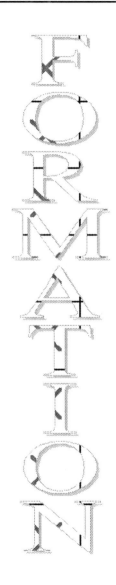

FORMATION

Chapter 1

*"I looked on my right hand, and beheld, but there was no man that
would know me: refuge failed me; no man cared for my soul."*
Psalm 142:4

Chaos

I was sitting on the couch at home watching television—at least
"home" is what it was supposed to be. Mom and I had just moved
back from Texas, and we were temporarily staying at my Aunt Ann's
house. Down in my gut I knew that moving in with her was a bad
idea, which time would certainly confirm. I tried to stay out of the
house as much as I could. Basically, I slept and got dressed there. There
was always some chaos or drama brewing.

To prove the point, one of those infrequent times when I was there,
minding my own business, there was a frantic knock at the door.
Boom! Boom! Boom! Over and over again the sound of a banging door
rang through the house. It just so happened that day that Mom and I
were both at the house. Thank God, my aunt and her kids were gone.
My Mom was upstairs in our shared bedroom, barely able to hear the
knocks. Therefore, by default, I opened the door. By the sound of the
hysterical knocking, I figured something had happened or was about
to—again.

I jumped up off the couch, and rushed to the door. Boom! Boom!
Boom!

"Who is it?" I asked.

"Jake, boy. Open up the door."

To my surprise the origin of the hysterical knocking came from my Uncle Jake, a man of medium height with deep brown skin, broad in the shoulders, and erratic at the mouth. When I opened the door, he stepped in the house about three feet, but never allowed me to close the door. I recognized quickly that he was drunk, upset, and ready to blow.

"Where's your momma?" he inquired.

"Upstairs, Jake."

Before I could say another word, Mom had walked down the steps to the back door where both Jake and I stood. I could look at Jake and Mom and tell that something was about to go down. Jake's face was distorted with wrinkles of anger, and his breath reeked of alcohol.

"What's wrong Jake?" Mom said.

"Yevonne, I'm gonna kill him. This is the last time Daddy is gonna disrespect Momma."

As I watched with curiosity and fear, I noticed that my mother seemed to be a little confused by Jake's comment. But I knew for sure she was going to get to the bottom of whatever the problem was. You see, Jake was like a son to her, although he was really her brother. Somehow, over the years my mother had become the surrogate mother for my uncle. She seemed to be the only person that could calm him down and help him to be rational in a crisis. Without fail, every time Jake felt out of control, he would go to my mother.

Unfortunately, this would be a night that my mother could not stop Jake from being illogical and irrational. He had his mind set on his version of justice. He only stopped by to tell Mom what he was about to do.

It turns out that he had seen my grandfather in a rather compromising situation with another woman. My grandmother had recently died, and Jake felt that the situation had disgraced the family and his momma.

"The nigga couldn't even wait until Momma was fully buried," he cried angrily.

Some of the family believed that my grandmother had overdosed on pills and liquor. Others believed my grandfather had had a part in her death. My grandmother had suffered for many years in a very dysfunctional marriage. As the story goes, my grandfather seemed to take out his frustrations on her and his kids, so when she died the family seemed relieved. They were all glad that, at the very least, she would finally have some peace, though they would all miss her very much—especially Jake, the only boy in the family. Somehow, the family should have known that hell was going to break out eventually between my uncle and my grandfather. There always seemed to be some form of animosity between them, unlike the feelings a father and son should have for one another.

"Well, Jake, what are you going to do?" asked Mom.

"I'm gonna kill him, Yevonne. I'm gonna kill him."

Moving swiftly, Jake quickly backed out of the door, and in seconds he was speeding off in his long, blue Lincoln Town Car toward my grandfather's house. My heart was beating faster than the second-hand on the clock because my past experiences had taught me that my mother would intervene. I didn't want her to, but I knew she would. No sooner than this thought entered my mind, I found myself running with my mother to her car to chase Jake down. Because my grandfather's house wasn't too far away, the ride was short, but it was the most fearful drive I had ever taken. By the time we arrived, things had already gotten out of hand.

Mom pulled up right behind Jake's car, and she and I both jumped out. What happened next would scar me emotionally for the rest of my life.

"Come on out, nigga. You ain't gonna disrespect my momma. You killed her already," Jake shouted while banging on the front door of my grandfather's house. When he heard my grandfather coming to the door, he ran back towards his car and us. Suddenly, my grandfather appeared—drunk and holding a handgun. Impulsively, my mother jumped between Jake and him and began to plead with my uncle.

"Stop! Are y'all crazy? Jake get in the car! Please stop."

But Jake wasn't hearing it. He continued to verbally bash his father. I tried to grab my mother, scared that something was going to happen to her.

I screamed, "Mom, get back in the car! Mom please get back into the car," but she wasn't listening to me. Everyone seemed to be caught up in the moment. Without any warning, gunshots began to ring out. Bang! Bang! Bang! My grandfather was shooting at my uncle.

"Come on nigga, you gonna kill me, too?" Jake, feeling invincible, asked as he dodged the bullets.

"Mom get in the car, please get in the car!" I was crying at the top of my teenage lungs.

Mom was totally focused on my Uncle Jake, and I was in the middle of the street struggling to save her life. It felt like the wild, wild West, except we were in the middle of a prestigious black middle class neighborhood.

Bang! Bang! Bang! Shots rang out from my grandfather's handgun. Father and son, in the middle of a suburban neighborhood, were arguing like hoodlums. It was the most pitiful sight in the world. On top of that, Mom and I were right in the midst of it. As tears began to roll down my face, all I could think to do was continue screaming in my attempt to get her out of the way of the gunshots. I feared that she might get killed. What would I do then? Mom and I had experienced some crazy things up to that time, but nothing as crazy as this.

Luckily, the gunfight ended. My grandfather grew tired of arguing with his son and walked in the house. When Jake realized that there was no more fight, he drove off in complete frustration. Who was left standing in the middle of the street? Mom and I. We stood there for a few minutes looking at each other, trying to figure out what had just taken place. I am sure the neighbors were too petrified to come out to find out what was going on.

The next day after school, I walked over to my grandfather's house. As I stood in front of his house, I noticed the bullet shells. I picked a few of them up off the ground, not fully believing that the previous night's situation had actually taken place. The entire scenario was absolutely absurd. I was embarrassed and confused. This was one more family event that I just couldn't logically put together in my sixteen-year-old mind. My grandfather had actually tried to kill his own son, and my uncle had actually provoked it.

Not too long after that incident, I realized that I would leave Flint, Michigan, and the Johnson family forever. There was no need for me to be there. Everyone in my family seemed deranged. I loved my mom, and I knew that as a single parent she had sacrificed so much to raise me, but I had to leave her, too. There was no way that I would live out my life in Flint with the rest of my family. It would take two years, but I was determined to leave, no matter what.

Chapter 2

"Before I formed thee in the belly, I knew thee..." Jeremiah 1:5

I Am Pregnant

After several minutes of hinting around the issue of my mother's altered physical state, the truth was finally revealed in the family room of my grandfather's house. It was an intense and fearful moment.

"Mom, I am pregnant." After five months of hiding her pregnancy, my mother finally summoned enough courage to tell her mother the truth.

"You are pregnant? What are we going to tell your father?" my grandmother replied.

"Yevonne, we have to tell your father. Now."

It was a chilly night in September, and my grandfather had already gotten comfortable in his bed upstairs. Usually, no one wanted to mess with him after he was in his bedroom because if you bothered him, he raised hell. In that respect, this night would be no different.

My mother looks back on that short walk up the stairs to her father's room as the longest walk in her life. She could muster no sense that this experience would be positive or loving. As a matter of fact, she knew her life was about to change forever; she just didn't know how. After climbing the last step with her, my grandmother gently pushed my mother forward into a place of no return. My grandfather turned his head from the television and eyeballed my mother suspiciously. Time stopped for just a few moments. Then, with a dry throat Mom said,

"Daddy, I have something to tell you."

"What, Yvonne?"

"I...I'm...pregnant."

"Barbara, get her black a_ _ out of here before I blow her g - - damned brains out."

Immediately, he launched to the closet where he kept his gun. In tears, my mother moved away from him and backed out of his room. My grandmother quickly pushed my mother down the steps and shoved her out on the patio. My mother waited for hours, but no one came to the door. So, with reluctance, she tapped on the door, and my grandmother quietly opened it.

"Momma, I'm cold. Can I come in?"

"No, baby. You need to stay out there."

Soon my grandmother returned with a blanket and threw it to my mother. Without any words of encouragement, or even a hug, my grandmother slammed the door. Mom stayed on that patio until midnight, quivering and shaking in the cold, not knowing if she would ever be allowed into the house again. A little after midnight, my mother's sister came home from a date and found her there sitting all alone in the cold. Mom's only solace at that moment was the compassion of her elder sister. My grandfather had turned his little girl away in her most desperate time of need, and she stood there in the cold not knowing what was going to happen. All she knew was that she had nowhere to go.

It was to this woman that I was born—an insecure, sensitive, black teenage girl, who understood little about love or life. She was the second of seven children, and it seemed from the very beginning she was destined to be the family hero. Likewise my father, who was the eldest of four children, also took on the responsibility of being his family's hero.

Kenneth, my father, seemed to be a bright and enthusiastic teenager, but that was only on the surface. In reality, my father was just as insecure and unsure of himself as was my mother. So it would seem that my future wouldn't be so bright, given those circumstances. My mother loved my father, and he respected and adored her, but they were from two totally different worlds, separated by social class. My father was raised by his mother, who was poor, rebellious, and as wild as anyone could be. Therefore, he learned at an early age to survive in the streets and take care of himself and his brothers.

My mother, on the other hand, was raised by two alcoholic parents in a middle class neighborhood. The economic disparity between my parents was obvious, but they both seemed to carry the same hurt in their spirits. This may have been what drew them together during their high school days. I know they had no idea that a son would come from their first encounter, but that's what happened.

As a teenager, Mom did her very best to nurture me. However, it was a real challenge because she never had a very healthy model for rearing a child. Besides, Mom was only a teenager herself. When I was born, she struggled financially and emotionally to be a fit provider, often working one or two jobs to make ends meet. My grandparents did but very little, so, for the most part, she was on her own. For several years we survived off of government aid. Though times were hard for my mom, I was unaware of the extent of her struggle until much later in my life.

As a single parent, Mom did her best to give me what I, a black boy, needed. She was aware of her inadequacies, so she turned for advice to the Phil Donahue Show, a popular daytime television talk show, which, along with reading books on child-rearing, and exploring other avenues of information, helped her to break the family's sick cycle of child-rearing. Had it not been for such help and my mother's deep desire to give me a good chance at having a decent life, I believe I would have ended up a thug.

My father never helped my mother through the tough times of raising me. Rather, he decided to go his way, and Mom became my mother and my father. I was so used to this type of upbringing that I thought it was normal. Whenever Mom talked about my father, she would usually only say positive things. I can't remember a time that she talked negatively about him. No matter how bad things got, she never blamed our circumstances on him, so I didn't grow up hating him, but I sure was very curious from time to time about why he wasn't around. Without question, my mother's love was so strong that his absence never became a significant issue for me until later in my teenage years.

Chapter 3

"For I give you good doctrine..." Proverbs 4:2

Daddy

One thing I can say about my father is that I learned from some of his mistakes. Though he was never around to help direct my path, I learned an important lesson from his example: "Life is short, so live it with the end in mind." Kenneth Franklin Brown, my dear father, lived as if he had no end. At one point, I did believe that he was about to make a change, but his shadows caught up with him, his life was cut down quickly, and he ran out of time to get it right.

I just knew I didn't want to follow in his footsteps. It was by the grace of God that I had a good mother and a built-in sensibility that enabled me to draw that conclusion on my own. No one had to tell me not to follow in my father's footsteps; his absence and frivolous lifestyle communicated enough to me. The following is an excerpt from a book that he began to write about his life:

Kenneth Franklin Brown
May 22, 1951—December 31, 1988

"I sentence you to the Southern Michigan Correctional Prison for not more than 11 and 1/2 years, nor less than 1 year Mr. Brown. Do you have anything to say?"

The judge asked me this as he stood there looking over me, with those black glasses hanging over his nose. I thought to myself, "What can I say? Thanks for the time." Actually I was happy about the time, because it could have been much greater than it was. So many others who had preceded me weren't as lucky as I was. It seemed that they were penalized harder, because they had judges who were insensitive. So with as much sadness as I could employ, I replied to the judge, "No, your Honor."

I took my appointed seat, after which other inmates were receiving their due penalty for their charges. One guy received 10 years to 20, another 5 to 15 years. Yes, there was no question in my mind, I was lucky. But still afraid of what would lie ahead. For I had heard many stories about prison and what they did to guys my age. At the time I was only eighteen. Not really a bad fellow either. I was just caught up in the drug scene. I was putting that poison called Heroin in my arm. It began to control my life, taking over my way of thinking until it led me into the arms of Mr. Justice.

As I look back at my life, this was the beginning of a cycle that would be my life. Crime, drugs and the arms of the law...."

Unfortunately, my father was never able to break the cycle that he so accurately described. He learned bad habits from his mother and stepfather which, eventually, he chose for himself. He would later be murdered at the age of thirty-seven—still so young—as a result of this lifestyle.

My father had the world open to him, but he decided to keep going in a direction that would inevitably hurt so many, including my half-brother and me. In many ways it was good that he didn't raise me because there's a great chance that I may have turned out just like him. Destiny has a way of shuffling the cards that way. If one doesn't believe in destiny, then God, as I believe, saw it coming and moved him out of my life for a reason.

Though he didn't stick around to lend my mother a helping hand in rearing their little boy, my mother never was bitter about it. When I brought him up in conversation, she would always say something positive about him. If she couldn't say anything positive, she would always say, "Tubby, no matter what, Kenneth Brown will always be your father." Many times I didn't want to hear that. I couldn't understand why my so-called father was never around. He left an eighteen-year-old girl with a son to take care of and never made an effort to make a difference in my life or hers.

As I grew older and was exposed to other families, I began to resent the fact that my father was absent. We never had fireside chats or went fishing, bicycle riding, or to baseball games. I don't remember any time when my father took a real interest in the development of my character. It is only now that I realize that he didn't have much to give. Daddy was trying to figure the "man thing" out, himself, but he was doing it by surviving rather than by living. He never learned to live. Instead, he got caught up in the street game, and it never let him go. The excitement, chance, danger, and quick money had their grimy grip on his soul, controlling him and driving him to do everything that he did.

Now, my father wasn't a mean person. He was very bright and sharp-witted, and he was enjoyable to be around. He had a certain charisma about him that made him stand out in any group. I believe I inherited this from him; some call it charm. His charm saved his life many a day.

I enjoyed being around him when he visited, and I always looked forward to the next visit. Of course, those visits were very infrequent, but enough to help me remember the man who called himself my father.

I remember three instances from my youth when my father showed up to be the "minute-dad." One such instance was during the 1974 Christmas holiday when Mom and I were living on Eldridge Street, on the north side of Flint. At mid-evening we heard a knock at the door.

Mom answered it, and there stood my dad sporting an Afro and clothes like the ones from the '70's movie *Shaft*. I was excited to see him—after all, he was my father—so I leaped into his arms, and he gave me a big hug. I remember feeling his prickly beard on my face when he kissed me on my cheek. My father was a tall man of six feet and four inches, so he always seemed to tower over me. I thought he was a giant because I was so small. After he put me down, I looked up at him, excited by his big grin.

"I've got a surprise for you, Son," he said.

He reached behind his back and placed a wrapped box into my hands. I ripped that Christmas paper off and quickly popped open the box. To my surprise, it was an Evel Knievel motorcycle. Right there, in the dining room, I knelt down on the beautifully polished hardwood floor and ran that thing all night. I was obviously excited about the toy, but I was even more thrilled that my father was there with my mom and me. On rare occasions like this one, I would fantasize that they would get back together, but it never happened. One thing's for sure: no other present that year could have measured up to this one because this was a gift from my daddy.

Shortly thereafter, Dad kissed me on the cheek and was gone. It was a little discouraging to hear the words "Good bye," because I knew I wouldn't see him again for a long time. He gave me a hug and said, "I love you, Son. I'll see you soon."

It would be several years before I actually saw him again. During that breadth of time, I began to desire my father with a passion. There was only so much my mother could do to meet my needs. (I needed a man, my father, to teach me manly things, and Mom couldn't do that no matter how much she tried.) I often wonder how things would have turned out if my father's head had been screwed on right. Unfortunately, I'll never know.

Later in my teenage years, after briefly living in Texas, my mother and I moved back to Flint, Michigan. I was in the tenth grade. This wasn't a place where I wanted to be, but it was where most of our family lived. My grandfather was dying, and my mother wanted to be with him during the last stage of his life. By this time I had long put my father to rest. I never talked about him to anyone. My life consisted of my mother and me, and I had no reason to think differently. I was sixteen years old and had learned what I learned about manhood from the streets and from my uncle.

One day while I was just relaxing at home, I heard a knock at the door. I thought it was one of my boys, so I ran down the steps expecting to head outside. To my surprise, I realized that the man I hadn't seen for well over ten years was standing before me—my father. I didn't even know what to say or do. Slowly, I opened the door and said in a querying tone, "Daddy?" as if I wasn't sure that it was really he. At the same time, I was wondering why he was knocking on the door after being gone for so long. I wanted to say to him right then, "Mom and I are making it fine; just step back to your world, my nigga." Rather, I opened the door and plunged into his arms. It was a great feeling, being in the arms of my father, a feeling I was not sure of, but that felt right. He hugged me and politely pushed me back from him, bending down a little and saying,

"Hey, Tubby. How are you doing?"

"Fine," I answered.

Then he immediately asked about my mother. I told him that she was cool, too. Then he asked me to get her. I stumbled up the steps to tell Mom the unbelievable news. She didn't believe me at first. She had to see for herself, for which I could hardly blame her.

When she came down the steps and stood in front of him, I didn't see anger in her eyes; nor did I see insensitivity in his eyes. I saw two adults who seemed to still care for one another. In some kind of weird way I again wished—as I did when I was a child on Eldridge Street—that they could be together. After a brief conversation with both of us, he managed to talk my mother into letting me go with him, to which she finally agreed. I could tell that she really wanted me to get to know him.

Dad was driving a cab, a type of employment that seemed quite appropriate for his independent spirit. I walked with him to the cab and jumped in, on the passenger side. As I sat down, he looked toward me and began to tell me about his life. It seemed as if he was trying to connect with me, but I couldn't feel the connection right away. Then out of nowhere came,

"Tubby, I can't make up for all those years in the past, but I will be the best father I can be now."

I accepted the apology, but in the back of my mind I could never forget the times my mother and I struggled financially because of my father's lack of concern. After his brief soliloquy, he slammed me with the heavy news: he was married and had another son.

"Nigga you got a son, and you're taking care of him, but didn't take care of me?" the hot words filled my mind, threatening to spill out of my mouth.

"Hey, I want you to meet your little brother."

I remained silent thinking that I didn't have a big choice because I was already in the cab. It was hard for me to feel anything at the time; I just sat there not knowing what to say. My father had come back and brought with him an instant family. As he talked and drove, the time seemed to slip by, and soon we were pulling up to one the projects in South Flint, where Dad and his wife and son lived. When I walked through the door, my father kissed Cassie, his wife.

"Brandon, I want to introduce you to your big brother," Cassie said.

He looked at me with his five-year-old eyes as if to say, "That ain't my brother." I was just as shocked as he was. Although this was all new, I actually became a little proud of the possibility of being a big brother. It was rational to me. Brandon would have what I never had—a big brother.

"Hey, Brandon, What's up?"

"Nothin," he reluctantly replied.

"Brandon is your name, huh?"

"Yeah. What's yours?"

"My name is Nevlynn, but you can call me Tubby."

I guess that was enough conversation for him because he didn't say anything else. My father seemed to be proud of the moment. Here were two of his seed standing side by side. We were probably the best things he had ever accomplished.

I could tell that Daddy was getting fidgety, so with little emotion and less finesse we were off to the next place.

"Brandon, you wanna go with us?" my father asked.

"No! I wanna stay with my momma."

Brandon didn't seem to have a real trust in our father, which I could tell that Daddy didn't like at all. At any rate, we were off in the cab again. Daddy took me home and promised that he would be back the next day. Surprisingly, he did make it back to the house the next day and many days following that. He and I spent a lot of time together that summer and into my senior year in high school. However, as I approached graduation, we spent less and less time with one another. I think the novelty wore off, so he didn't pursue the relationship with me the way he had in the beginning. But the time that we did spend together was invaluable to me. I learned a lot about him, and I found that we had a lot in common, which was weird to me. I wondered how it was possible for two people to be so alike without ever spending time together? It was a mystery then and continues to be one today.

My father never graduated from high school. Both he and my mother attended the same high school, but she was the only one to graduate. I believe my mother graduated as a result of middle class performance pressure, which my father didn't have. Dad's mother was wild and loose. She never took the time to impress on her kids the need for an education. Rather, she smoked marijuana and drank liquor with them. This is where his survival motif probably kicked in. Making money and getting rich was the key to success in his mind. School was a waste of time; there was much more fun to be had in the streets. By not having to raise a child as Mom did, he had it easy. This was where my mother and father parted roads. As much as Daddy loved my mother, he knew that he would be no good for her. He forcefully broke off all contact with her. Mom couldn't completely understand it at the time, but he actually helped her more than anything.

Ironically, as he gained entrance into my life he felt it necessary to encourage me to stay in school.

"School is important; stay on in there," he would say.

Of course, my mother had already drilled this in my head at any early age, so I had never thought about dropping out. I knew that my mission was to complete high school, then proceed directly to college.

"If you don't, you'll end up in jail or something. Trust me," Dad would often say.

I knew he wanted the best for me in his own special way, but he just wasn't able to model that way of life for me. Luckily, I had a mother who could.

Another major momentous occasion for me was my graduation. I looked forward to seeing my mother's and father's faces when I walked across that stage. More than anything, I wanted my father to see me because I sought his approval. I remember sitting with my classmates in the auditorium, waiting for my name to be called. I knew my father was in the audience. It was the one thing he had committed to do for me for which he actually came through. Within minutes my row was called up to receive its diplomas. I felt good standing there knowing that my dad was watching.

After going through about a hundred names, it seemed, I finally stood at the top of the stage waiting to be called next.

"Nevlynn Lewis Johnson," the announcer said.

I stood up straight and smiled with pride as I glided across that stage. I reached out for my diploma knowing that 'independence day' had finally come. As I grabbed that paper, all kinds of things crossed my mind. First of all, I was so glad to walk across the stage, and better yet, glad that I was still alive to experience such a moment. My next thought was that I had made my mother proud of me. So many things had happened in the first eighteen years of my life, and now I was seeing the product of my perseverance. Mom and I both knew that circumstances could have turned out so much different. I believe, in my fathers quiet moments while watching me cross the stage, he felt the same way too.

After all of my classmates received their diplomas, we were asked to stand for the recessional. We walked to the appropriate aisles, about to recess, and, through some stroke of destiny, I walked down the very aisle where my father was sitting. As I passed Dad, he stood up and reached his hand out for mine in complete happiness. When my hand touched his, I knew that he was giving his approval of me. It was an overwhelming experience. I didn't think about it much then, but as I think about it now it makes me cry. This was the first time in life that my father had ever kept his word to me. This was the first time that he had ever seen me complete something. It was also the first time that I ever realized how much my father's smile and approval impacted me.

I had so wished that he had been a more intricate part of my life. I needed a father at times when my mother couldn't understand. For instance, I didn't know how to date. I had to learn the hard way. I learned about sex from my mother. She did a good job, but I would have preferred learning from my dad. When I got into fights and had to learn how to defend myself, my uncle taught me, not my father. When I needed a man's shoulder to cry on, I didn't have it, so I just didn't cry much. All of those feelings and emotions were bottled up inside of me because of my father's absence. But he came through for me at a critical time in my life. My father watched me graduate from high school. That event was an honor and a memory I'll never forget.

After graduation I went to the Air Force and lost touch with him. Actually, for almost one year I didn't even think about him, so caught up was I in my new military life. Then on January 1, 1988, I got a telephone call from my mother notifying me that my father had been murdered. I was nineteen years old; the person who killed him was the same age as me. He and my father had gotten into a heated argument which ended in violence, and he shot my father multiple times while my dad was sitting in his car. According to the paper in D.C., Dad was pronounced dead upon arrival at the hospital. I sat in my dorm room that day confused and wondering what to do next. My dilemma was answered quickly, however, when, as his next of kin, I was asked to take charge of his funeral arrangements. How ironic that the son he left behind in his quest for life was the one who had to bury him. My father was dead, with all the dreams he ever had for himself and all the dreams I ever had for us wiped away in seconds.

To this day I miss him very much, especially since I am a father now who appreciates parenthood as a true and irreplaceable gift. Fatherhood is wonderful, but it is also very challenging. The responsibility alone is very intimidating, so I can understand just a bit why my dad turned from it. I know my father was not a man when he was eighteen years old; he wasn't even mature enough to make the right decisions about his own life, let alone a family's. Despite this, I still wish he had been there with me. He never saw me grow a beard or lose teeth. He never saw me throw up in the bed when I was sick. He never had the 'pleasure' of changing my diaper. He never experienced the pain of watching me cry. Finally, my father never saw his wonderful grandson. How tragic! He took his life for granted. Then again, maybe he wanted it that way. At least now he is at rest. Dad will never have to face his fears again. They are dead with him.

Chapter 4

"There is a way which seemeth right unto a man, but the end thereof are the ways of death." Proverbs 14:12

My Hero

"Now, you know Big Jake was your uncle. That nigga loved you too...Now, I know who did this. I wanna get those niggas."

I nodded my head agreeing with Wild Man. Wild Man was one of my uncle's best friends; they grew up together. He was like a part of the family. Jake was the leader in the relationship, and, for the most part Wild Man was the follower. There was a time in their youthful lives when they were inseparable—one in every sense of the word. But as they grew older, they seemed to grow apart. When Jake got married their relationship began to change, but one thing seemed to stay the same: Wild Man loved my uncle and wanted to defend him to the end.

"So, Tubby, do you wanna get these niggas tonight?"

"Naw, Wild Man. I can't do that."

"Aaight, I understand...I got this! I'm a creep on those niggas."

"Cool, then, I'm about to go talk to Tracy. I'll see you later, Wild Man."

"Hey, Tub, I am proud of you. Big Jake was too. You got outta here, and you doin' good. Love you man!"

I walked away from him knowing that life had really changed, especially for me. Some years prior to my being in the Air Force, I might have been game for joining forces with Wild Man to kill these murder suspects. But at that point, I just couldn't do it. I had a new life outside of Flint and the thug life that Wild Man was notorious for. As much as I recognized that there was injustice in the murder of my uncle, I couldn't be God and repay murder for murder. It just wasn't my place.

Moments later, I joined my aunt in the house and spent a short time talking with her about my dear uncle. The whole thing seemed surreal.

"Tubby, you know Jake loved you so much."

With my head down, I replied, "Yeah, Tracy."

"Really, Tub, you were real special to him, and I am sure he would want you to have this."

We were in their bedroom. She reached into a jewelry box and pulled out a watch.

"Here. Take this to remember him."

Reluctantly, I reached for the watch, taking it from her carefully and placing it in my pocket. I didn't have the courage to tell her then, but that watch didn't mean anything to me. I wanted my uncle back.

Just days prior to this family time of mourning, my uncle was standing outside of his house alive. Moments later, shots rang out in a drive-by specifically intended to send him to his grave. Four shots to the back did it. As his wife was watching from the window, he grabbed for the gate in the driveway and struggled to stand. With no strength left, Jake hit the ground, lying in a pool of blood.

I was stationed at Barksdale Air Force Base in Louisiana, when I was notified by my mother that Big Jake had died. It was a terrible moment for me. I was nineteen years old and had just buried my father in the same city six months earlier. I was tired of death and violence, especially in my family. I was the only Johnson boy left to carry on a legacy of hope, but for some odd reason I feared that death was slowly creeping toward me like a family curse or something. I didn't know what to do but keep moving on.

Jake was a very meaningful person in my life; in many ways, he was my hero. Though he had a mean streak and a knack for the street life, he was also kind, protective, and considerate of me. I accepted him just as he was, despite his obvious flaws because he was the only male image in my life. When it came to Jake, I sort of ate the fruit and spat out the seeds.

The times I spent with him were crazy and often outlandish because he did things that most people just didn't do. Some scared me, others made me laugh hysterically. No matter the moment, if I was with my uncle I knew there was going to be some excitement. He took a stroll on the dark side many days, and sometimes I didn't know if he would return, but somehow he always did—except that last time.

I remember being in the car with him when I was much younger. We were driving back to his house from a car parts store. As we were driving, a yellow street light flashed, an obvious indication that it was time to slow down. (Jake was a fast driver, so yellow lights always upset him, especially if he couldn't beat the light before it turned red.) This time, while we sat at the red light, there was a white guy parked next to us. Casually, the white guy looked around and happened to catch Jake's eye. He appeared to be a middle class white man, who obviously had no idea that in the street, staring too long at a person could result in a physical altercation. Unfortunately, he quickly found out that Jake had a street mentality when Jake yelled some very profane words at him. The man never returned the insult. As a matter of fact, he quickly turned his head trying to act like he had never seen Jake. That just upset Jake all the more, so he said, "I know you heard me, white boy. What you lookin' at me for?"

The man continued to look straight ahead, avoiding my insane uncle. Without notice, Jake jumped out of his car and walked to the man's car with brisk force and quickly grabbed at the driver's door. The man looked up at Jake with fear. His face was red; he was obviously confused, though not any more so than I. I couldn't understand why my uncle took the situation so far. Luckily for the white man the light turned green, and off he screeched leaving tire marks on the pavement. Had that light turned green any later, Jake would have pulled that white man out of the car. It scared me to think that someone would fight over a stare, but at the same time, I admired the power Jake had to instill fear in that man. It was a sick sense of control and power.

When Jake returned to the car he seemed proud of what he had done. I got the idea that he really liked scaring white people, particularly men. It wasn't a good thing to do, but I guess for him it was a way to get white folk back for the rejection he felt by white society at large. Regardless of Jake's behavior, I still loved him with all of my heart. His mental health and behavior out on the street never seemed to be of any consequence to me. Funny as it may sound, he often reminded me to be different and better than he was. Deep down inside, I know he knew that I was cut from a different cloth. Jokingly, he would remark about that too—

"Hey school boy. What you learned lately?" Or he'd say, "Aye white boy, with your proper talkin' self." Though to some these things may sound demeaning, I really knew they were his way of saying that I was different. He wanted me to be different, but he was afraid that I would lose my blackness or something. I knew that was what was inferred in many of his comments.

He would often sit and talk to me about Texas or Georgia, and get himself all excited about the possibility of his leaving little ole Flint, Michigan—but he never left. In the end, Flint was all that he ever knew; it was all that he would allow himself to experience. Caught up in the madness of the street life, he knew its ways and its people, and they knew him. So I guess it was a little intimidating for him to go somewhere new, where no one knew who he was.

When I would come home on leave from the military I would drive straight to Jake's house where the conversation would usually begin and end the same way:

"Aye, nigga. You have grown up so much. You think you can whoop me now?"

"No Jake, I can't do that."

"I know that's right. I will always be able to whoop your a_ _, no matter how big you get."

"I know, I know," I would agree.

He would always follow that salutation up with—

"Where you live at now? Your mamma told me that you were in Mississippi or something like that. Tell me about it."

As I would begin my stories about my new-found life, he would always interrupt me.

"Tub, take me around to Wild Man's house."

Or it could be anyone's house, store or junkyard. It didn't matter just as long as he could show off his nephew who had made it out of Flint.

"Damn Jake," his friends would say. "Tubby has gotten big."

And his reply would always be, "But not big enough to whoop my a_ _."

For some reason, that was always the major factor. He was right. I never was able to whoop him. Even if I could, I wouldn't have had the heart to do it. There was so much humor and honor in knowing that my uncle would always be tougher and bigger than me. It was all a part of the hero complex I so lovingly bestowed on him. I don't know if anyone loved my uncle the way I did. I miss him to this day. I miss the times we went out to buy clothes. I miss the times he'd ride me around town in his big trucks and stylish cars. I miss the times we wrestled and laughed at each other. Although his life ended in tragedy and violence, I will always remember him as my hero.

By the way, Wild Man, my uncle's friend, was sent to prison for murder. As it was told to me, he killed a woman in her apartment. Seems that he was out of control. I can't help but think about what my life would have been like had I followed his suggestion to kill my uncle's suspected murderer. I am glad that some way, somehow, I turned away.

Chapter 5

"They will build houses and dwell in them..." Isaiah 65:21

Our New House

Living in apartments and with relatives can really be a burden, especially if you want your own space. After a few years of being transient, my mother got fed up. She wanted her own space for us. I believe she heard about a new government program that enabled low-income families to purchase homes in low-income communities. This was a dream come true for Mom because we were on government aid and had no real chance of buying our own house, so she applied. After a few months, her application was approved, and within a year we were moving into our brand new house at 321 E. Eldridge.

Prior to moving to our new house, when I was about five years old and curious about everything, Mom had taken me for walks around the neighborhood and pointed out various things to me. She even walked me to the school I would be attending. She made me feel very comfortable about our new community, which made me anxious to move into our new house. Although the neighborhood was completely different from the community my grandparents lived in, I was still able to deal with it. I know Mom was excited too. For the first time, she was able to claim a piece of property as her own.

We didn't have a car when we moved to Eldridge, so we would walk to the corner store to buy our groceries. On the way, I would ask

Mom all types of questions. I know I drove her up the wall with most of them, but she never let me know it. Mom was always very patient, encouraging me to ask questions. That is the main reason why I learned so quickly. Our new house was the beginning of a whole new life. As far as I was concerned life couldn't get any better.

It wasn't long before I met a few of the many kids that lived in the neighborhood, Two or three of whom are unforgettable. Paul, my buddy who lived around the corner, attended Dewey Elementary School and cub scouts with me. Erika lived down the street from me, and was real smart. Curtis was a straight up thug who had a perm in his hair. Curtis was forever bullying the 'brothas' in the neighborhood. He just thought he had it like that. While living on Eldridge, I had a lot of fun. I might have only been five years old, but a lot happened during the two years that followed.

Mom and I lived directly behind my Aunt Ann's rental home. A few of my friends and I would play kickball, tag, and other fast moving games between her garage and our back yard, a large space where we could hang out and get into a little mischief sometimes, too.

Once one of my friends and I watched or read a story about getting rich by finding gold or oil, and we convinced ourselves that gold or oil had to be underground somewhere around the backyard. So we picked a spot behind my aunt's garage and started digging. Night and day we would secretly get together to shovel out dirt, determined to find something. I think we dug every day after school for almost a week until the hole was so big that we could both stand in it and had to help each other in and out of it. We would have continued digging, but one day my aunt's landlord came by and, for some reason, went to the back of that garage. He was extremely angry when he saw the crater in his backyard. We got into so much trouble.

I was too young to understand why he was angry. Couldn't he appreciate our desire to get rich, I thought. After all, we would have paid him back for any damages after we successfully retrieved the treasure. Unfortunately, that never happened because my mother forbade me to ever go back in that area. She also banished me from using the shovel for a while. Sometimes I wonder if anyone ever found the treasure behind that house. It had to be there; I just knew it!

I always had a knack for making friends with adults. I enjoyed my peers, but there was something about older people that really intrigued me. I was able to communicate a lot easier with adults, it seemed.

Well, one day I was riding my bike when I realized that we had neighbors who were a different color than I was. The neighbors were white, or as I later learned to call them, Caucasian. This was the first time that I really began distinguishing between races. The entire neighborhood was predominantly black at the time, so I thought it peculiar that there would be white people living there. They were very nice people, and they never bothered anyone. They seemed to be very secure with the atmosphere too.

Eventually, my curiosity got the best of me, and after getting permission from my mother, I wandered across the street to meet them. There were always pigeons on their property, so I figured I could make some new friends and get to play with their pigeons.

After the initial visit, I continued to make myself a regular guest at their home. My new friends were an older couple, probably in their sixties, and I began to like them a lot because they were like grandparents. They were patient and very kind, and they loved to talk to me. We would talk about birds and a lot of kid stuff. I felt that they really were interested in me, unlike my own grandparents. Really, that's all I remember about them. In that entire neighborhood, there was only one white couple, and they were the nicest people you'd ever want to meet. They left an impression on me that I'll never forget, and it is probably due to their desire to reach out to me that I never grew up with a lot of animosity for white people.

We had other neighbors who were not as nice or as friendly as my white neighbors. I learned real early that a few of our inner city neighbors were dangerous people. Often, I would hear gunshots or see a lot of fighting on the streets. Usually, when the fights got out of hand, I would walk into the house and watch from the window. Much of this type of craziness became an exhibit for everyone in the hood. It got so bad that people would actually run outside to see a fight, like an HBO special. This I could never understand. Chaos seemed to always lie nearby; all it took was the wrong look, and it was on. As early as five years old, I became aware of genocide. Watching my own people get caught in this cycle of violence was awful. At the time, I wasn't aware of the effects, but now, as I look back on it, I understand why so many kids in the city grow up numb to violence.

If you were going to be out in the hood, you had to buy into the philosophy, which was all about getting yours and protecting yourself. I remember vividly that some first graders were bringing knives to school because they felt they needed to protect themselves. It was so chaotic, and there seemed to be no one around trying to stop it. Violence became the norm in the city of Flint. It was routine to hear about people getting shot or stabbed. Really, it was typical to actually watch someone breaking into a neighbor's house. Life was just crazy like that around Eldridge. Everyone was doing their own thing, with little regard for anyone who might get hurt in the process.

Many people in the community sought to escape poverty and oppression through the sale and use of drugs, but ironically, instead of escaping, they remained trapped in a hideous cycle of emotional and psychological poverty. To gain respect and feel classy, pimps, dealers, and players drove around showing off their fancy cars, but very few realized that they were only perpetuating societal stereotypes, and even fewer saw the downward spiral that their lifestyle guaranteed.

I knew it was getting bad when my mother started explaining what needles and cocaine pipes were and why they were lying in the street. She always looked disgusted explaining those realities to me. It was as if she wanted to wish it away, but that wasn't quite possible. The subculture that surrounded us was a lot bigger than she was.

I was attending Dewey Elementary School where every kid in the neighborhood attended. Usually, all of the kids walked to school, the in-thing to do. One day at school I got into an argument with this brotha, and he became real angry with me. He wasn't very big, but he looked tough enough. He wore a perm in his hair and knew words that I wouldn't dare use. This was Curtis, whom I mentioned earlier. Curtis was the bully of my childhood.

He seemed to love his bully title. Curtis looked like a grown man in a six-year-old body. Whether his appearance was a ploy to punk everyone out or not, it worked well with me. I tried to stay clear of him. After the in-school incident we were to meet outside for the fight. I didn't want school to end that day, but time flew by quickly. Before I knew it, the bell had run, and I knew it was my time to meet the grim reaper. At six years old, I was sure I was going to die, and everyone around me knew it.

After waiting in the school for a long time, I finally had enough courage to walk outside. Curtis wasn't there. I felt relieved. All the kids were outside waiting for this battle of the fists. Since he didn't arrive to welcome me to the party, I felt it was my obligation to end everyone's curiosity. So, not feeling a need to stick around, I smiled at a few people and began to walk home quickly. As soon as I began to walk away, the bully showed up with his entourage.

He cut me off, then came at me and swung, but he missed. I think I hit him, and that really ticked him off. Then the unthinkable happened: he pulled out a knife on me. He swiped at me and cut my coat. It was then that I decided to use my legs rather than my arms. I turned around and ran for my life. I figured that if I ran he would get his applause and leave well enough alone, but he didn't. Curtis waited for an opportune time to get me again.

For a long time I was badgered and badgered by this kid. He was really getting on my nerves, but I didn't have the courage to stand up to him. Avoiding Curtis the bully became my full time job. One day when I was walking home from school, I stopped at the store. Little did I know that Curtis was at the store, too. We spotted each other immediately. As I backed out of the store Curtis and his crew started chasing me. While running I was thinking, "I have to make it home. I know it will be cool when I get home." I knew in my heart that if I didn't make it home, it would be all over for me.

Tears began to well up in my eyes because I couldn't believe that this was happening. I was completely petrified, but I managed to run fast enough to stay several yards in front of them. As I was approaching the homefront, the most beautiful scene in the world caught my eyes. My uncle was standing in front of the house. My uncle was a tough guy, and everyone in Flint knew it. I thought to myself, "If I can just make it to Big Jake, he will take care of these bullies." I called out to my Uncle Jake with the loudest scream possible for a six-year-old. At first he just looked at me and refused to budge. He just stood there like a statue. I wondered if he had heard my screams of fear or had seen me running for my life. Jake wasn't reacting to my plea for help.

Soon, I ran past my uncle and straight to my front porch, where my mother was standing. I looked down the street to see if my enemies were still pursuing me. Indeed they were, but something was about to change. My uncle jumped in front of this mob squad, picked up Curtis, and slammed him on top of his car, just hard enough to make a point. Then Jake said,

"Turn your little butt around and go home, and don't come back 'round here no more—you hear."

Jake also said a few other things that were not becoming for an adult to say to a child, but it worked. As soon as Jake put him down, Curtis and his crew ran for their lives down the street.

I began to feel relieved, but the feeling fizzled when, a few moments later, I heard Curtis yell back to my uncle that he was going to get his daddy. Although I felt some temporary relief, I knew that there was going to be a war on Eldridge, and all because of me. Just then, my uncle called me to come to his car and told me his philosophy of the hood.

"Boy, you don't have to run from anybody. Pick something up and start swinging on the toughest one in the crowd. If you knock him out, then no one else will mess with you." That advice has stuck with me for life. But what if I didn't knock the toughest one out, I wondered. Jake never explained that and I never asked. I was merely relieved that my problem seemed to be solved, until I saw a black Cutlass Ciera rolling around the corner.

An angry brotha stuck his head out of the car window and began to curse. I looked in the car, and there was Curtis. I wanted to wail on him right there, but I was too scared. The guy driving stopped the car and asked, "Who was f _ _ _ _n' with my son over here?" Curtis immediately pointed to Jake. Slowly Jake turned around and said, "I did nigga." That man's face dropped like someone had cut it off.

"Jake. Jake Johnson. Is that you?"

"Yeah," he replied.

"Jake man, what's goin' on over here? My son said he was threatened by some man."

My uncle politely told him what had happened, and that ended the situation. Curtis' father apologized and drove away, slapping his son in the back of his head.

It felt great; the bully was put down and in his place. I never had any more trouble out of him. I was telling everybody about what happened and getting big props. Moreover, I learned something very important about the street. You didn't get respect in the hood by your intellect or your grade point average. It was pure brute. If you couldn't fight, talk a good game, and hold your own, you would be eaten up.

Chapter 6

"There is a time for everything, and a season for every activity under heaven: a time to search..." Ecclesiastes 3:1, 6

Tent Revival

I wasn't raised with religious rules or creeds as a child. For much of my early childhood, I had no idea what religion was. For example, I was not taught how to pray, nor was I taught scripture. I am sure my mother respected God, but a particular religion or faith was not lived out in our home. I would say that we were basically moral people.

I was about six years old when my mother started attending a local community college—not for a degree initially, but to get money from the student grants. After she started hanging out with some serious students, however, she discovered that she liked college, so what began as a con to get money developed into a serious quest for self-improvement through education.

During this time, tent revivals were big in the area, and I asked my mother about the big white tents in neighborhood parking lots. She said the people who went to the tents were Holy Rollers, church people who were religious fanatics. One day the Holy Rollers pitched an enormous tent that took up half the field around the corner from our house on Eldridge. Just the idea of people having church outside in a tent and falling out and shouting tickled Mom and my Aunt Ann, and they began to make fun of the Holy Rollers, playfully mocking them from time to time. Eventually, their playfulness led them to curiosity, which prompted them to visit. Much to their surprise, they ended up giving their lives to the Lord, which shocked and scared both of them. When my mother returned home that night, she seemed a little different. Though I didn't quite know what the difference was, I knew something had happened to her. The next night my mother and I headed for the tent together. This time my aunt was nowhere to be found—scared off, I guess. Mom dragged me, which didn't concern me too much until we walked in and I realized that I didn't know anyone there, and that the people seemed to be so different than me, which added to my fear.

Mom and I sat down. Still feeling uncomfortable, I began to check out the surroundings. Not only had I never been anywhere like this, but I was actually pretty scared as I watched the people talk, jump, and scream while the minister preached. Not knowing what to make of it, I was ready to go. Then all of a sudden the preacher asked the lost folk to come forward to accept Jesus Christ and receive the Holy Spirit. The next thing I knew, my mother was walking both of us toward the preacher. As we approached the front of the line, the organist began to play, and the preacher walked over to my mom and placed his hands on her forehead. Immediately, something began to happen to Mom. Without notice, she fell to her knees and, with her eyes closed, she reached out for something like a person. Her arms and hands were stretched out wide and high. Then I heard her mumble words. Next, she leaned backward. I began to worry, thinking she would hurt herself. Then Mom started shouting and crying. By then, I was at my breaking point. I reached for her to save her, but these strangers kept me from touching her. They kept telling me that she was okay, but she sure didn't look okay to me. I was convinced that something was wrong with her and that these people were the enemy for traumatizing my mother. So intent was I on saving her that I had to be restrained.

Mom remained in a trance-like state for a long time. I waited as long as I could, then broke the human restraints and ran to hug her. But still raising her hands to something I couldn't see, she didn't grab for me. That was my clue that something was really wrong. I thought to myself, "What did these mean people do to my mother to make her not recognize me anymore?" Just when I was about to lose it, Mom came to and told me she was okay.

"Tubby, I felt him," she said with conviction.

"Felt who?" I questioned.

The preacher and the people in the tent seemed happy about this whole episode. They were clapping and shouting. Some people were dancing too. But joy escaped me in this absurd and foreign place. Finally, the service ended, and Mom and I went home. After she put me to bed, I lay there thinking that I wanted nothing else to do with that tent or anyone associated with it.

I don't remember Mom and Aunt Ann discussing the revival much after that. My Mom seemed to be affected by it, while my aunt seemed to ignore her experience. My mother was no longer the same woman. That revival was the pivotal point in our lives.

For a while, my mother and I attended the church that had sponsored the revival, and she learned about praying and reading the Bible. I would watch her pray at home and speak in tongues, which freaked me out. But it was obvious that God had begun working in her life. I could see a change in her decisions because prior to the tent revival, my mother had been willing to take dangerous chances with her life. The revival had probably saved our lives.

I can't say that I am an avid tent revival supporter, but I can say that it seems God uses tent revivals. Had it not been for a few people who were willing to take a chance pitching a tent in a rough neighborhood, my mother might have remained a lost soul. And who knows? I might have turned out to be some bully on Eldridge.

Eventually, I began to learn the ways of the church as I attended church services with my mom. Besides high emotionalism, there were things to learn about the Bible through the preaching, which was done by the pastor and other men.

I believe this is where I got the first glimpse of what my future might hold for me. One day my mother needed to go to the tent to see someone. As we drove up, the pastor greeted us, and Mom got out of the car and began talking to him. I wasn't feeling too well, so I hung back in the car. To my surprise, the pastor leaned over and poked his head through the car window on the side where I was sitting. "Hey son," he said. "You look like you are going to be a preacher some day."

Where he got that idea, I didn't know, but he planted a seed of thought that stayed with me throughout my early adult years. I admired this pastor, but I had no concept of what it meant to be a preacher. Later on, however, I would know.

PART TWO

New World Order

Chapter 7

"The Lord said to Abram, "Leave your country..."
Genesis 12:1

The Big Move

I guess it was time for a change. Maybe I should have seen it coming. My mother's attitude about life was changing for the better. At the community college that she was attending, she was being exposed to another world, and she began believing that there was a life outside of Flint, Michigan. Mom had taken a liking to a middle-aged woman professor at the college who, in many ways, became a surrogate mother to her. This woman gave my mother the moral support to pursue great things, which encouraged my mom to apply to Michigan State University. My mother had experienced a spiritual transformation, and now a mental transformation. It was a wonderful process for a woman who lived much of her life not believing in herself.

Things worked out. The next thing I knew our furniture was packed, and the house on Eldridge was completely empty. Mom was accepted to MSU, and decided that it was time for us to move on, even though Flint was the only life she had known.

This move was about more than college for my mother. It was also about her desire to give me a better life. Mom knew that if we continued to stay on Eldridge, my world would be too small. I was seven, so I couldn't fully conceptualize what was happening. All I knew was that I was leaving my friends, the ditches I had dug out, the bully, the drug needles, and my white neighbors. What else could there be? And why move? As I look back, moving was the one of the best things that ever happened to me. My mother had the courage to make a move that would not only change her life, but mine as well. Some of the kids I grew up with in Flint are in jail now or dead, or just hanging out on the street because they fell into the traps of the 'hood. I praise God that a spiritual and psychological transformation took place in my mom. As a result, both of our lives were saved from the pit of poverty and obscurity.

We packed the green LaSabre, our only means of transportation, and drove slowly from our green and brown house on Eldridge, headed to East Lansing, Michigan. As we drove away from our government project to an unknown future, I had mixed feelings. Life was sure going to be different without the exciting and dangerous events in North Flint.

As Mom prepared herself for this transition, she knew that she would have to confront her father with the news, but she was very nervous about this because my grandfather was a predictably violent man. I think she knew in her heart that she was not going to get the support she needed from her parents—she never did—but she still wanted to give it a try, hoping that they might be supportive.

My grandparents lived in a bourgeois black neighborhood on the south side of Flint that had been abandoned several years earlier by a white community when blacks started moving in. Mom and I drove somberly to their house. Not a word was spoken between us as I am sure that Mom was trying to think of the right words to say to her father. Her lifelong ambition had been to please him, so this attempt was very important to her. When we arrived, Mom told me to get out of the car. I obeyed, walking a step behind her toward the front door. She rang the doorbell, and my grandmother opened the door. Very few words were exchanged as we walked in. I had a sickening feeling that something bad was about to happen. Grandma walked straight into the kitchen and stood by my grandfather, who was busy drinking a bottle of Canadian Mist. Mom and I stood several yards away from them near the patio window. The atmosphere was cold; they felt distant from us, as though they didn't want to be bothered.

For a while my mother just stared at the both of them, probably too scared to say goodbye. Then the inevitable happened. She spoke.

"Mom and Daddy, I just wanted to say goodbye before we left," she quietly began.

Immediately my grandfather spewed out his bitter venom to discourage Mom.

"I don't know why you are taking your black a_ _ up there anyway. You're leaving your house and don't even have a job. The only way you're making it now is because of Tubby," he said, referring to welfare.

From that point on I knew it was bad news. Granddaddy tried to kill her will and spirit with his belligerent words, but it didn't work. After his verbal onslaught, Mom grabbed me, and we walked away and got into the car. Once we were safely out of my grandparents' house, Mom wept. I tried to console her as best a child could, but to no avail; the tears kept running down her face.

I believe this was when I really began to despise not only my grandparents, but also the rest of my family. They all seemed to use Mom; they never came around until they wanted something from her. I got tired of seeing her hurt, but she didn't seem to mind. As a matter of fact, she welcomed it.

We backed out of the driveway and headed towards our new life. I had fears that we would never make the trip because the car had more problems than it was worth. We'd drive for a while on the freeway; then it would stop. Mom would get out, telling me to stay seated, and there on the dark freeway she would fix the problem. She was determined to get to East Lansing, which was only a forty to fifty-minute trip. But due to the car problems, it took us about three hours to get there.

Once there, we drove through the city looking for Spartan Village, the new apartment community where we would live. Then I heard Mom say, "Here it is. This is our new place." I drew closer to the car window to look around, but it was really too dark to see anything. All I knew was that we had finally arrived, and I was ready to see our new home. We drove around the complex and pulled up in a parking lot facing our building. We got out of the car and walked up the steps to our new home. Mom opened the door.

All I could think to say when we walked in was "Wow!" It wasn't spectacular at all. As a matter of fact the apartment was a dump compared to our house, but as a child I didn't think that way. I guess it was the newness of the environment that excited me. Mom seemed to be excited too, and that helped. Immediately, she showed me around our new place, a tour that took less than three minutes because our new home was small, but comfortable.

As the evening progressed I got hungry. Usually, my mother cooked all of the meals rather than taking me to restaurants, so I was wondering how we would eat since the dishes were packed. We didn't have any food either, since Mom hadn't bought the groceries. Intuitively, I knew that she would figure something out, but my stomach didn't share this knowledge. A little later she ordered some food from a place called Dominos. Shortly thereafter, a man knocked at the door. When Mom opened it, a white man was standing there wearing a red, white, and blue outfit with a hat that had a domino on it. When he handed my mother the pizza, its smell immediately filled the small space of our new apartment. After paying him, Mom placed the pizza, the first she had ever bought me, on the table and fed me what seemed like the best food I had ever eaten. Prior to moving to East Lansing, I had only eaten pizza once, but from that time forward pizza became my favorite food. My experiences were already changing. No delivery person was ever going to deliver a pizza on Eldridge in Flint.

After eating, my mother put me in the bed and partially closed the door to my room. My stomach was filled, and I was tired, but not too tired to notice that my mom looked a little worried. Whenever I saw her this way I wanted to help, but there wasn't much I could do. Somehow, I knew things would work out, though. I believed in my mom.

My Uncle Jake and his crew arrived—ghetto loud—to deliver our furniture the next night. After quieting them down, Mom directed Jake and the crew to our apartment. It took them about three or four hours to get us moved in. Then Jake gave me a big hug and waved goodbye. I stood on the porch and watched him drive away. I was going to miss my uncle a lot.

Turning back toward the apartment, I was impressed with it, now fully furnished, though living in a place where I didn't know anyone felt a little funny at first. Mom and I were strangers. Soon I made the adjustment to change, and Spartan Village became my new home. I began familiarizing myself with it by searching every corner. My mother, on the other hand, still seemed a little unsure about things, probably thinking to herself, "What in the world have I done? Was I crazy or something? Did I do the right thing?" She must have thought things like this often. But she kept on going, and I have always admired her for that. She didn't let fear keep her from moving on.

Chapter 8

"...Parthians, Medes and Elamites: residents of Mesopotamia, Judea and Capadocia, Pontus and Asia, Phrygia and Pamphilia, Egypt and the parts of Libya near Cyrene..." Acts 2:9-11

Diversity

I learned a lot about the world while living in East Lansing. In Flint, almost everyone I knew was black in a city that was split between the poor north side and the more affluent and white south side. Things were predictable in Flint. In East Lansing, everything was different, including my neighborhood.

Spartan Village, where a significant number of students lived while they attended school, was a housing project owned by Michigan State University. The residents came from many different countries, which proved to be a benefit to me. Our neighbors on one side were from Iran, and on the other, from Kalamazoo, Michigan. Below us lived an interracial couple—the father was from Nigeria, and the mother from Brazil. Their children were my friends. They grew up speaking Swahili, Spanish, English, and French fluently. I had a real good friend from Iraq, whose name was Sinan, who lived across the way from me.

Nick was Italian and real cool, and he and I played a lot of basketball together. I had a crush on a girl named Leslie, who was Native American, African American, and white. I thought that she was the best thing since sliced bread. I had another friend named David, who was from Mexico, and he also had a crush on Leslie. This didn't set well with me, but we still got along. There was Kwame, from Ghana. When Kwame moved away, he continued to stay in touch with me through letters.

Kwame's mother always complained about how Americans messed up the English language. The word 'pizza' was an example. She pronounced it as it looks and sounds, but Americans pronounce it *pete-sa*. This really annoyed her, so I had to be very careful of my enunciation around her. Kwame's family was great; they had a lot of pride in their culture and were very secure in their identity.

I had another close friend, named Nehru, who was from India. His family introduced me to a variety of new foods, some of which I still enjoy. When I met them, I had never seen nor eaten a mango, a fruit they ate quite often. One day when I was visiting, I asked Nehru,

"What's that red and yellow thing on the cupboard shelf?"

He began to tell me about it. His mother must have overheard our conversation because she pulled the fruit from the shelf and cut it for us to eat. When I took my first bite, I was hooked. I remember going home and telling my mother that I had eaten a mango. I asked her to promise to buy me one the next time we went to the store. Unfortunately, when we went shopping we found that the fruit was too expensive. Things like that bothered me, but I tried to understand. I was introduced to a lot of new things, but couldn't appropriate many of them because our family lacked the money.

The diversity among my neighbors broadened my tolerance for and flexibility with people. In most of the relationships racist remarks or attitudes did not surface because we appreciated our differences and celebrated our similarities. Those who were most intolerant were white Americans, for whom racial prejudice was always an issue, owing, I believe, to their elitist attitudes. I was very aware of cultural differences among my friends, but I never thought these differences should be a reason to limit the friendship. It seems that my neighbors from other countries saw things the way I did and even more, they appeared to really enjoy life in America as a learning experience.

There were some bad experiences at Spartan Village, particularly with a white southern family that lived downstairs from us and they, unfortunately, embodied many of the South's stereotypical negative attitudes. Though they lived among so many different people they remained exclusive with their relationships. Mike, my buddy, was their son. JD, his dad and a straight up bigot from the mountains of Tennessee, was loud and ignorant, often making derogatory comments based on race and ethnicity about our other neighbors. Ironically, Mike and I became friends of sorts, with his dad's permission. I think JD allowed the friendship and my visits to his apartment because this gave him a chance to try to make me feel inferior to him and his family. Had it been up to JD, he would have sent blacks and all the international students back to where they came from. He was intolerant and blatantly arrogant.

Mike was older than I, which was the one of the reasons I enjoyed being around him. He was also one of the first kids I met in the complex. At the time, *Star Wars* was a popular movie, and Mike and a close neighbor collected all of the ships and action figures. Our time was taken up mostly by indulging in our Star Wars fantasies, role playing and such. It was fun, but there seemed to always be a little tension between Mike and me, especially when his other white friend was around. We were never as close as many of my other friends, but I tried to keep an open mind about him. If he was willing, I figured I would be too.

The time came when Mike's family decided to move away. I believe JD had graduated from school. During this transition, I noticed a major swing in Mike's attitude toward me, from friendly to mean and insensitive, just like his father, so I figured I'd return the favor. Since Mike was bigger than I was, fighting was out of the question; instead, I decided to have verbal warfare with him. This went on for some time until we stopped speaking to each other. I simply made up in my mind at the age of nine or ten that I didn't need abuse in my life from anyone, so I just stayed away from him.

On the day of their move, I was sitting in a tree watching them. Mike had taken his father's keys and begun to play with them outside. He noticed me in the tree and began to make a few negative remarks toward me, but I ignored him. Then all of a sudden, he tossed the keys in the air, and they fell directly into the sewer. I laughed so hard that I almost fell out of the tree. Mike got scared because he dropped the keys in the sewer, so he decided to take it out on me.

"Stop laughing, you jerk."

"I can laugh if I want to," I shot back. Then Mike said the word that made my body cringe.

"Nigger!"

I knew it was on then. I started to climb down from the tree, ignoring all of my previous logic regarding his size, but before I could get down his dad came outside. He asked Mike what the commotion was all about. He told his father that I was laughing at him because he had dropped the keys in the sewer. I acknowledged Mike's comment to his dad by laughing again, louder this time. Then his father looked up at me and said,

"Shut up before I kick your little black a_ _."

At that point I was pissed off, but I was out numbered, so I stayed in the tree until my mother came home, watching for a good while as Mike and his father tried to get the keys out of the sewer.

As soon as I saw my mother, I jumped out of the tree and ran up the stairs to tell her about my confrontation with JD and Mike. Immediately, my mom grabbed a Louisville slugger and headed to the steps. My mom is a short woman, no taller than 4'11" and couldn't have weighed over 165 pounds. I had seen her get into plenty of fights but it never occurred to me that she had enough spirit to declare war on a man that stood 6'4" and weighed 350 pounds.

Mom moved swiftly to the ground floor and headed straight for Mike's house. She knocked loudly on the door. When JD came to the door he was very reluctant to open it. As a matter of fact, he opened the big door, but stood behind the screen door to listen to what my mom had to say.

"If you ever touch my baby or say another word to him, you'll have to deal with me. You understand?" she demanded.

JD looked at her without commenting. I think this made her even angrier, but she walked away. When we got back to our apartment, Mom told me to stay away from Mike and his bigoted dad. I was shocked at my mother's bravery, and scared of what the outcome could have been, so I listened to what Mom said and took her advice one step further by staying in the house. By the end of the day, Mike and his family were ready to move, and I walked out on the porch to watch them pull off in their moving truck. In a funny way, I was sad to see them go, but I knew we could never be friends because his mother and father taught him values that kept him from getting along with the other kids in Spartan Village. This family lived in an international smorgasbord and never learned to appreciate it. How sad. I wonder what his world is like now.

Another incident occurred with a rather unique white family. The mother, a single woman, was raising her natural daughter (Melissa) and an adopted daughter, who was black. For some reason, I don't think Melissa ever got used to the attention that her mother gave to Jennifer, her new black sister. Melissa's mom was a big woman who loved to cook tacos, which I always made sure to grab a few when I dropped by. Anyway, I was playing around in the back field minding my own business one day when Melissa started to tell me how to conduct myself. Two years or so had passed since the incident with Mike and JD, so I was around eleven years old, and Melissa was thirteen. I guess Melissa felt that her age gave her special privileges, but I decided to ignore her petty comments. When she continued to nag me, however, I let her have it. We argued back and forth for about three or four minutes. Then all of a sudden she broke out and called me a 'nigger.' Again, someone white had decided to insult me with a racist word, so I reached back as far as I could and smacked Melissa directly in her mouth. Her mouth started bleeding because she wore braces. Melissa ran home crying, but I didn't care. I felt vindicated.

That 'nigger' word was really starting to get out of hand. As I moved into middle school I began to hear it often. Attending a predominantly white suburban school had its disadvantages, and name-calling was one of them. 'Nigger' was always the word that ignited a fight. Mom told me to ignore words, but some words were hard to ignore, and 'nigger' was one of them. I knew I wasn't a nigger, but it was the point and the motive behind the word that hurt the most. I knew it was wrong to hit Melissa, and several other kids, but at the time it felt right. Now I wish I could apologize to them all, particularly Melissa. My hitting her didn't change the fact that she felt that way toward me.

Many of the negative racial situations that occurred during my childhood were initiated by educated white people, something I could never understand. While pursuing an education, many of these white people remained racist and prejudiced in their hearts. They took classes with black people, rode buses and shopped at the same stores as blacks and other people of color, but it didn't matter to them. I began to realize that my color carried with it a negative mark that I didn't create, but that I had to live with.

Chapter 9

"...but money is the answer for everything." Ecclesiastes 10:19

Deerpath

After a few years, I guess Spartan Village lost its flavor and we moved to Deerpath, a brand new apartment complex in East Lansing. Deerpath was located on the edge of a very nice residential area, and directly across the street from the wealthiest community in the city. With a setting completely different from Spartan Village, Deerpath was intentionally developed to be an aesthetically appealing community for families who wanted to live in the suburbs, but couldn't afford it. The rent was adjusted according to the income of each household, which made it very affordable for many people. Again, Mom hit the jackpot. Similar to Eldridge Street, we were able to live in a new complex without paying high-end prices.

Living in this new community brought new challenges for me, now twelve years old and becoming more conscientious about my appearance. I wanted to buy all the new styles of clothes with popular name brands, but this was a major problem because Mom and I were on a very low budget. Simply put, we couldn't afford all of the popular fits of the day. In addition to that, I also became very embarrassed about using food stamps. Some of my friends would go to Seven Eleven with me, and as they paid for the items with cash, I would pull out food stamps. "Hey what are those?" they'd ask. I don't think I ever came up with an answer. I usually ignored the question. I wasn't mad at Mom for our situation, but I knew something had to change for me. Mom was doing the best she could. I figured I could help out a little, so I found ways to make money.

Money hadn't been such an issue for me before, but now I was becoming conscious of my surroundings and of economic disparity. I had lacked this awareness in Flint and at Spartan Village where some people had cars and others rode the bus, but everyone seemed to be on the same economic level. The people that lived in this new neighborhood, however, were in the upper middle class, and it was apparent that we were on a different economic level than they, which was weird until I learned to get used to it.

I did notice that there were few to no black families living in this community, and I wondered why. I knew that there were wealthy blacks living in East Lansing somewhere; I just had never met them. Reflecting on this, I wanted a different future for my family and me, including my mom. I didn't want my kids growing up seeing needles, broken bottles, cigarette butts, or trash in the streets. Further, I didn't want them growing up on welfare. Once again, my world was expanded. I saw that I had choices in life. I didn't have to live in government housing for the rest of my life.

Besides the economic differences that existed at Deerpath, there was also a color issue to deal with. Many of the surrounding communities were created to keep blacks out of them, among them one named White Hills where a white wall surrounded the entire development. I knew there were no black families living there. The very name of the development indicated the value system of the community. This was hard to deal with at twelve, but I found ways to handle it. The older I became the more I realized that race was a systemic evil. I dealt with it at school, out of school, in restaurants, and even in my relationships with my white friends. I never used this as an excuse to get angry with anyone. Simply, I recognized the race issue as a part of life, whether I liked it or not. The diversity in East Lansing helped shape me, but there was definitely a line drawn between race and class.

Chapter 10

"Go to the ant, you sluggard; consider its ways and be wise."
Proverbs 6:6

The Work Ethic

'Ingenuity' and 'creativity' became my middle names during my Deerpath years. When I put my mind to something, I found a way to get it done. I found out early that excuses got me nowhere; the best way to succeed was to simply get the job done.

One day, a friend of mine by the name of Scott caught the bus with me to downtown East Lansing. We were both headed to look at some new clothes for school. It was summertime, and our goal was to have all of our school clothes picked out and bought before the beginning of the school year. I had reached the conclusion that shopping with my mother was getting me nowhere because she seemed to be drawn to clothes that made me look like her little baby again. Starting middle school was no joke, and my mother's choice of cute blue light special clothes was not going to ruin my chance at impressing my peers.

I liked downtown East Lansing with its long sidewalks packed with storefronts and a variety of specialty shops. Bright colors and neon signs highlighted each store and restaurant. Just the atmosphere made my heart race. I felt independent and responsible.

Scott and I decided to shop at the Izod clothing store. Everyone was wearing Izod and Polo apparel, but Izod's clothes were expensive and way out of my range. I considered myself lucky when I bought just one Izod which would have to last me the entire year.

When Scott and I walked into the store, I knew we were being watched, but I decided to overlook this because I was there to shop. By this time, I had already developed a sense that my color put me at a disadvantage in white communities. My black friends and I were always under suspicion, and it was common for a store attendant to follow me throughout the store. When white students walked in the store, they were given freedom to shop. This would irritate the heck out of me, but there was very little I could do about it.

As Scott and I walked in the store, we began to look at the new styles of Izod shirts. Bright colors for boys was cool: pink, purple, yellow, and orange. As I looked at the shirts and other clothes, I could just imagine myself dressed up in all of the outfits I liked. Imagination is as far as it went that day, but I was determined to change that. I was going to get an Izod shirt, and soon.

I found one that I really liked. It was short sleeved, with purple and white stripes. Prices for shirts like this one started at $17.50. "Whew," I said. The cost of that shirt was too rich for my blood, and this was the cheapest shirt in the store. Scott and I left the Izod shop and walked down the street to a shoe store where I found a pair of Pro-Ked shoes. They were white and black, and I really liked them, but I couldn't afford them either.

After adding up the costs of these two items, I knew that I would have to generate some revenue to get the clothes I really wanted. This is when I learned about the work ethic. It was by far the best thing I learned during my adolescent years.

After talking to Mom about my desires, she helped me come up with a number of creative ideas to help me move forward. Within hours, I was out trying to make things happen. Those Pro-Keds and that purple Izod shirt were my motive for working, so the work didn't seem bad at all because I knew there would be a reward at the end. I knocked on every door in our complex, soliciting work.

"Hello, my name is Nevlynn, and I am trying to make some money to buy a few things. Would you like me to take your trash out for twenty five cents?"

If that didn't work I asked if they would allow me to wash their dishes for a dollar. If that didn't work, I asked if I could clean up their apartment. If that didn't work, I would ask if I could wash their car. I knew that someone had something for me to do, and I was determined to find it.

Eventually, I built a strong clientele, and the money began to pour in. Quarters turned to dollars, and dollars turned to five dollars. The money kept adding up. Soon, it seemed that opportunity had found me. My reputation spread throughout the complex, and I became a household name in Deerpath. Adults would stop me in the parking lot and ask me to do odd-end jobs for them. They usually paid me more than I requested too, which made the jobs all the more enjoyable.

One of my jobs was not too pleasant. A blind woman in our building with a retriever guide dog had heard about my services and asked her daughter to hire me to walk the dog. The part I hated about the job was picking up the dog's waste with a pooper-scooper, but I tolerated it because I knew it would pay off in the end. It also helped that I began to like the dog.

I had several jobs that summer, including a paperboy one. The paper route was fun and paid more than my other jobs, but it was very time-consuming. Mom had to help me with that one because it included several residential areas in addition to our complex. As the jobs progressed, so did my savings. I was even able to open lay-aways at the Izod shop and the shoe store where I found the Pro-Keds. This was a good time, and I worked hard. Things were just about to get even better.

Toward the end of the summer, Scott and I were riding our bikes from a friend's house and passed through a nice residential area located directly behind Deerpath. All of a sudden we saw something that appeared to be money lying in the front yard of someone's house. Before I knew it, Scott had jumped off his bike and run straight for the stash. Trying to maintain my balance, I leaped off my bike, closely trailing him. Indeed, what we saw was money, and Scott and I picked it up as quickly as we could and jumped back on our bikes. We peddled more vigorously than usual, screaming at the top of our lungs with excitement. Within minutes, we were pulling up to Scott's house. Once there, we jumped off of our bikes—frightened, happy, and excited—and ran in to tell Sharon, his mother, about what had happened.

We had never found that much money before.

"Momma, come down stairs!" Scott screamed.

"What in the world is wrong? Are you all right?" Sharon asked.

"Momma, we found a lot of money outside."

Immediately she walked down the stairs with a curious look on her face. When Sharon got downstairs she calmed us down. She asked us to put the money on the kitchen table. When we did, she very coolly counted it for us, carefully thumbing through every dollar.

"Where did you find this money?" Scott's mom asked.

With excitement, Scott and I told our miraculous story. Then she told us that we would have to take the money back.

"What if someone has lost this money? Surely they are looking for it right now. You two get into the car; I am going to take you back to the house so we can return the money."

My heart dropped to the ground. Scott and I looked at each other and just knew that our efforts were for naught. Begrudgingly, we slowly got in the car and directed Sharon to the house. To our surprise no one collected the money.

Sharon then drove us back to the complex and split the money evenly between Scott and me. It turns out that we found $150. When I got home and told my mother the story, she just smiled, but then she asked the same question that Scott's mother had asked. Luckily, his mom was nice enough to explain the whole story to my mom. Now it was official. I was seventy-five dollars richer. As the summer was coming to a close, I had made enough money to buy that Izod shirt and the

Pro Keds. I even had enough to buy a few extra items. I felt that these were the rewards for my hard work.

I learned a lot of important lessons that summer about the work ethic and the value of money. It was essential for me to learn that everyone works for what they have, and that if I wanted something, I had to work for it. To this day, I have benefited from the lessons I learned in Deerpath, and I have never had a desire to take something that wasn't mine. I am glad that Mom encouraged me to work. I also learned that opportunity and money find you when you get focused and your heart is right.

PART THREE

Lone Star

Chapter 11

"Reckless words pierce like a sword…" Proverbs 12:18

Texas, Here We Come

As much as I enjoyed my stay in East Lansing, I was pretty excited about moving to Houston, Texas. I had been to Texas once before, and had had a wonderful time, but I knew it would be nothing like East Lansing. I would have to make new friends and find new employment for myself. Actually, Mom's hope was to find a good paying job. What she would make in the professional mental health field was going to surpass any money she had ever made before. If things went right, I wouldn't be doing any more paper routes.

My mother had finally done it. She graduated from Michigan State University with a Masters degree while raising a kid. At twelve years old, I didn't fully appreciate her achievement, but she had really accomplished something that many welfare mothers never do. She persevered to the end. My Mom was head strong about making something of herself, and she did it, at the same time instilling in me the same passion. I knew as we were leaving Michigan that she would display the identical perseverance in Texas that she had shown at Mott College and at Michigan State. She was ready for the next challenge, and I guess I was too.

After her graduation we prepared to go to Texas. With our relatives in line to take things off our hands, it didn't take long to give away our furniture and other belongings, thus making it easy for Mom to look forward and not backward. All we took to Texas were our clothes. Since my Aunt Linda worked for Continental airlines in Houston, we were able to purchase cheap tickets and affordably fly to our new home.

The plane ride was smooth. I looked out of the window the entire flight, captivated by the thought of a plane actually staying in the air. The clouds were blue, and the sun was shining. It was a wonderful day to fly.

During the flight, Mom had a contemplative look on her face. I could only imagine what she was thinking. After all, this was another big move for us. As a single mother she was probably wondering how she would support both of us. At times like these I wondered where my father was. I was never able to see him make a decision for the family. I never saw him sweat moving furniture from one apartment to another. Mom was the only model I had when it came to decision-making. Once again, she was teaching me life lessons about taking risks.

We talked very little on the airplane because I was preoccupied with the flight, and Mom was probably preoccupied with her decision to move. She reached over and put her hand on my leg to make me feel secure, I guess, and then I felt the plane land. Knowing that we were out of the air and on Texas soil was pleasant. Aunt Linda met us at the airport and gave us a big hug, then hurried us along to the luggage pickup. Once we were out of the airport and in the car, Aunt Linda told my mom that we would be living with my Aunt Ann until Mom was able to get on her feet. Ann was the same aunt who lived behind us on Eldridge Street in Flint.

In less than thirty minutes, we arrived in a small hick-looking town with which I was totally unimpressed, but what could I do? Immediately, I began to feel strongly about living with Linda because I knew she lived in a much better place. But Mom and I were sticking together.

Linda parked the car across from Ann's apartment complex and pumped the horn. Ann, who had moved from Flint to Humble about one year earlier, came outside with a big smile, happy to see us, my cousin Keisha right behind her. Linda left soon after she helped us take our luggage up to Ann's apartment. In less than three hours, we were new residents of Humble, Texas, by the looks of which I knew I was going to have a very interesting time.

It wasn't long before Mom enrolled me in Humble Middle School, located less than five minutes from our apartment complex. This school was predominantly white, with kickers being in the majority. All I knew about kickers was that they were country music-loving cowboys, and when I saw them at school, that impression was confirmed. Most of these guys chewed awful smelling tobacco. I was never able to understand why anyone would want to do that.

At the other end of the spectrum were the black kids, who were in the minority. During lunch we all sat together, which helped us to grow into a close, tightly-woven community. I learned quickly that we all had to look out for each other because Humble was notoriously a racist city. Usually at school, the white kids spewed racist words at us, and the word 'nigger' was as commonly heard as the name Jack. A lot of fights got started because of it. There was so much tension that we had trouble at times concentrating on our studies.

Unlike East Lansing, Humble was very homogenously bigoted, and folk outside of the white kicker culture were ostracized. Since that included the entire small black community, I felt very uncomfortable there and hated it. Had it not been for the other black students, I would have lost my mind. Many people in Humble were also proud to be affiliated with the Ku Klux Klan; it was even rumored that a KKK post existed there. Because of this my mother was scared for my life and didn't want me to play outside at night. I couldn't run around scared all the time, I reasoned. I was aware of the possible danger, but I needed to live, to, so as much as I could, I tried to avoid trouble. In the meantime, I worked hard developing as many friendships as I could.

During lunchtime at school, there was one game that black and white students played outside together, called 'Suicide.' Students would form a human line against a wall while one or two people would throw a tennis ball or racquetball hard at the wall. The object of the game was for someone in the human line to catch the ball—nothing short of an act of bravery. But if this brave person failed to catch it, he or she would become a moving target who could only escape by touching the wall. If you touched the wall, you were safe. You had to be pretty tough and quick to play Suicide.

One day a friend of mine named Tracy asked me to play. I was a little unsure about it because blacks were in the minority. There was already tension between the rednecks (the lower echelon of the white community), kickers, and us. So I was trying to play it safe. But really wanting to play, Tracy walked away from me and jumped in the game. I couldn't bear watching him all alone out there, so I joined in. There I was in a group of twenty white boys with tension in the air and the brute competition of this game, which certainly didn't help matters.

I caught a ball that bounced back with force from the wall. Then I threw that ball toward my opponent. Things were going well at this point. Now, it was Tracy's turn. I jumped to the other side of the group, and I watched Tracy catch a ball and throw it with precision towards one of the rednecks and hit him. Even though Tracy was playing by the rules, it just didn't set well with that group that a black boy hit one of their own. Immediately, the boy turned around and called Tracy a black nigger.

Tracy was a well-mannered and well-dressed young man. He did pretty well in school, too. For the most part he was well respected by all of the black students, but Tracy had a little problem. He had a tremendously bad temper. Tracy was always looking for an excuse to fight a white kid; that day he got his wish. Tracy looked at me and I looked at the one who called him a nigger. As we met each other's eyes, there was a quiet commitment that took place. I knew that Tracy and I were going to have to fight.

Tracy approached the boy who called him a nigger while I stayed behind him to take anyone else who would jump in.

"What did you call me white boy?" Tracy asked.

"I called you a got-d_ _ _ _ nigger," the redneck answered.

The game came to a quick freeze as everyone's attention was focused on Tracy and the redneck. Other rednecks and kickers began surrounding us. We were absolutely outnumbered. Tracy lifted his balled-up fist to fight, but before he could land the first punch, I ran up and grabbed him and said, "Man lets go. It's not even worth it." I pushed him to look around at the group surrounding us, and reluctantly he pulled away.

Why that redneck had to make comments after that, I'll never know. "You had better get on outta here nigger," he scowled. His entourage spewed out a few more comments and laughed. As we walked back into the school, I noticed that Tracy was fed up. It seemed that he was going to break. There was a lot of hostility and frustration in him, more than usual. We sat down in the lunchroom, and Tracy looked at me and promised me and everyone at our table that he was going to get that redneck before the end of the school day. I was new in the group and didn't really know Tracy that well, but I had a sense that he meant what he said.

As usual, when the bell rang we walked each other to class and looked forward to the next bell. In class, a few kids talked about the confrontation. I was getting a little paranoid, thinking that everyone was plotting on Tracy. After class, I hooked up with the crew to prepare them for a possible brawl. When the five-minute bell rang, I began to look for Tracy, but he found me first. He told me, "I'm gonna whoop that redneck before the next bell rings." I tried to talk him out of it, but it didn't work.

He walked down the hallway, and within a few seconds the two antagonists bumped into each other, and the fight was on. But before Tracy began to swing, he asked the white kid an odd question: "Did you call me a nigger at lunch?" I don't know if Tracy was trying to allow this guy to redeem himself or not, but the kid didn't catch the hint. Without hesitation the boy answered, "Yeah, I called you a nigger." The next thing I saw was Tracy's fist in this boy's face, and the boy's face bobbing back and forth like a punching bag. Tracy lit into him like it was a heavy-weight bout. In less than five minutes, Tracy had managed to whip that guy to a pulp. Blood was all over the hallway. All the frustration and anger that Tracy had inside of him was released on one person. I actually pitied the guy, which may explain why I tried to pull Tracy off of him. I couldn't quite manage it though. Tracy was determined to kill him. Had it not been for the principal, I really think that Tracy would have killed him. The more blood he saw the more he fought. It was like he really enjoyed seeing blood pour out of the boy's body.

That same day Tracy was suspended from school. As justice would have it, so was the white kid. Tracy proudly walked out of the school with a smile on his face. The next day we black students talked about the fight at the lunch table. In some weird way Tracy became the hero of the hour. He had done what all of us wanted to do, given a similar situation.

In retrospect, it is sad to think that we, the black students, were disliked so much due to our race when we were only in middle school. Why would any kid in middle school be more concerned about hate than mathematics or science? I hate that I had to experience that awful day. Racism and prejudice were alive and well in Humble. We weren't liked, and that was no secret.

Chapter 12

"So justice is driven back, and righteousness stands at a distance..."

Isaiah 59:14

Tubby

One day during the winter, while we still lived in Humble, my mother and Ann had to go to the local retail outlet, Target. Mom asked me to stay home to watch Ann's eight-year-old daughter, Keisha. I really didn't want to do it, but I had no choice, so after they left, I watched television and tried to stay away from Keisha, who always tried to get me in trouble. I figured she wouldn't lie on me if I just stayed away from her. Time passed quickly, and the shadow of nightfall fell, peeking through our window. Mom and my aunt had promised that they wouldn't be gone for long, but as the hours passed, I sat on the couch wondering what could have happened to them. Why were they taking so long? Did the kickers get them? Or were they snatched up by some weirdos? I knew something was wrong, but I didn't know what it was.

The telephone rang. I picked it up. "Tubby, Ann and I are in jail." It was my Mom on the phone. "Tubby, I don't have a lot of time to talk, so listen. A policeman wants to talk to you. Tell him what you know." I agreed, and a policeman got on the phone immediately.

"Who is this?" the officer asked.

"My name is Tubby, sir."

"How old are you?" asked the officer.

"I am twelve."

"What is your mother's full name?"

"Yevonne Bertha Johnson."

"Where are you from?"

"Michigan."

I felt like all that was missing was a dark room and a bright light. It seemed as if I were being questioned and possibly prosecuted over the phone. My hands were sweating, and I began to worry that if I said the wrong thing my mother and my aunt would never make it home. I was completely nervous.

After the questioning—as if that were not enough—the policeman told me that he was sending an officer to the apartment to meet me. He told me to expect a Humble policeman within ten to fifteen minutes, and that it would be important for me to open the door. I wanted to do everything right, so I got Keisha and explained everything to her and had her sit down somewhere to be easily seen. Then I waited. Sure enough I saw a flashing light, then heard a quaking knock at the door. "Were they gonna bust in on me?" I wondered. Quickly I walked to the door, unlocking the locks and turning the knob and opening it. I looked straight into the eyes of a very large, white policeman.

"Hello son, what is your name?"

I told him my name, but he didn't seem interested. It appeared that he was looking for someone else. He walked in the apartment, curiously scoping it.

"Does anyone else live here son?" he asked

"No sir, just my cousin Keisha over there."

As the policeman turned his stone cold, suspecting eyes down toward me I didn't know what was going to happen next. Within a few seconds, he asked me a rhetorical question.

"So, you're Tubby, huh?" Surely, he knew the answer to that!

"Yes sir," I answered.

"Okay. Thank you for your cooperation. Now, close the door and lock up."

"Yes, sir."

I wondered, "Did I answer the questions right? Was I nice enough? Will my mother ever come back?" No kid at that age should have to worry about such things.

I would later find out that the Humble police were trying to link a suspect to my mom and aunt, for some reason thinking that the two women were protecting the guy. Here's what had happened. Ann had gotten into an argument outside of Target with a white man about a parking space at the same time that the police were trying to apprehend a black suspect. The argument led to my aunt's and mom's arrests, which later made it easy for the police to suspect them of being accomplices of the suspect—some big black guy who had run through the Target parking lot.

When the police questioned my mother, she told them that she had a son named Tubby. Since my nickname, given to me at birth when my grandfather noticed that I was chubby, is usually tagged on a fat person, the police assumed that "Tubby," was their man. It was hard for them to believe that the person that my mother was describing to them was her young son. They simply refused to believe that my aunt and mother had nothing to do with their suspect, so the only way they could disprove their hunch was to visit the apartment to meet me, Tubby.

Several hours later, there was a familiar sound in the door—keys. I had never been that excited about hearing the rattle of keys before. Soon, the door opened and I saw my mom and Ann walk into the house. They were free. Mom was back, and I was happy.

After consoling Keisha and me, they began to talk about suing the police department. They seemed to have a good case, but they never pursued it. After that incident, we were all determined to leave Humble and its bad treatment of black people. Justice was not real for blacks in good 'ole Humble, Texas.

Chapter 13

"It is good for a man to bear the yoke while he is young."

Lamentations 3:27

Westheimer

One day Ann went out exploring the city for a new apartment and found a place inside the city limits of Houston. She came home excited about taking us to see the new complex. The possibility of leaving Humble was extremely exciting to me. I hated living in that place. The new apartment was located on Westheimer, which continues to be the busiest street in the city of Houston. There was access to buses and plenty of opportunity for a variety of employment. Most importantly, there were plenty of kids of all races to play with. I found that this situation was very much akin to East Lansing, and that unlike Humble, Houston was a diverse city. There were Mexicans, Puerto Ricans, Africans, South Americans, Iranians, and many other nationalities and ethnic groups. Without question, this new environment was a definite improvement.

Mom enrolled me at Paul Revere Middle School. Considering the cultural dynamics of the area, I thought that Paul Revere would have been an ethnically diverse school, but I was completely wrong. Paul Revere was a predominantly white school, but the kicker and redneck elements were less dominant. Rather, there were preppie and valley girl constituencies whose parents were successful professionals. There was a small population of blacks at the school, and just as in my previous school experience, they usually all stuck together. Though there was a difference in location, it seemed that many of the same issues were present.

I developed some quick friendships in the complex, which made life much easier. I met a kid by the name of Mikey who was white and seemed to have a philosophy on life already. Mikey's mother was an exotic dancer whose late night to early morning work hours pushed her son to grow up quick; he smoked and cussed and lived on the fringe of society, basically raising himself. One thing he learned how to do well was play pool, probably one of the most positive things he did. But on the negative side, he learned how to hustle, and he hustled at the pool hall where he would take money from grown men like candy. (Mikey was real good at what he did.) It was just unfortunate that no one was helping to steer his gift into something more positive. We had a lot of fun together, but I always felt sorry for him. I had it bad with my living situation, but his was much worse. Mikey never seemed to be happy. I could tell that he was searching for something.

Then there was Tony. He was a year younger than me, but he was a big guy for his age. This brother was really into his health and body-building, which was of no interest to me. But weight lifting was Tony's world. Over time, he became like a little brother to me. We were real tight. He lived with his stepfather and mother one of few middle class black families I knew. As the story was told to me, Tony's mother had met his stepfather at a bar that he owned. They dated for a while and then got married. His mom, a very attractive and well-dressed woman, was considerably younger than his stepfather.

Tony had a few stepbrothers, one of whom was a stripper. Because his stepfather had an interesting philosophy about sex, Tony was destined to be ushered into adulthood in a most unhealthy way. His stepfather established a ritual for all of his boys when they all turned fifteen. For their birthday present he would bring them to his club and hook them up with one of the prostitutes. So Tony and his brothers were literally ushered into the world of sexuality by prostitutes paid for by good old stepdad. At the time, he was barely twelve, but he bragged on the day that some woman would freak him at his father's club.

Tony always struck me as one of the confused black brothers because he always identified himself with the white prep group. These were sophisticated upper middle class white folk, who never associated with blacks unless it was to make fun of them. Several times, I watched from a distance as this white group mocked Tony and his culture, but he never quite caught on. It irritated me because I knew Tony's heart. Because his family was able to afford the same lifestyle as many of the white students, he felt out of place many times with the black group at school. It was a real dilemma, probably more for me than Tony. I guess after living in Humble, I was a bit untrusting of my white peers. Because Tony was my friend, I didn't want to see him get hurt. Eventually, we had many discussions about his relationship with that group. Slowly but surely he began to see the games they were playing. Finally, he got hip to the situation.

Then there was Darryl, who lived down the way in the same complex. He was in high school, but we hung out a little. Every time we were together, Darryl, who had nude magazines all over his room, talked only about sex. This brother was fixated on sex. I liked girls, but I wasn't at the stage of life where I felt comfortable about engaging in sexual activity. Darryl was a very tall, dark brother. He was so dark that Tony and I would sometimes call him blue. He wasn't a handsome guy at all. I guess he knew how to lay the lines down because he had the girlies at his parents' apartment all the time. A few times Darryl would invite me to stay, and the girls were cool with it. Due to my fear of the unknown, however, I always backed out. Darryl never messed with me about that either. It was all good to him, either way.

Beth would have to be the next person I got cool with. Her family was temporarily living in the complex because they were building a new house. Beth came from a professional family that had moved to the United States from England. She had a very unique accent, and she was the finest white girl I had ever met. Unlike other white girls I had met, Beth was very friendly. As a matter of fact, she was very comfortable with dating black guys. For a while, we kicked it—nothing intimate, just good friends. Tony and the crew thought that she was a fox too, but none of them approached her.

One day on the way back from school, Beth was sitting on the bus, and when I got on she asked me to sit with her, so I did. There was a kicker on the bus who had a crush on Beth, but she didn't give him the time of day, which I'm sure he didn't like. As I walked to take my seat next to Beth, this Kicker rudely confronted me about sitting with her. I ignored him until he called me a nigger. What did he do that for? I lit into him like Tracy lit into that 'ole boy in Humble. I tried to put a serious hurtin' on the chump. We had a black bus driver named Willie. Willie was cool. He stopped the bus and ran down the aisle of the bus, grabbing both of us and making us sit in our seats. Then he lectured us for about two to three minutes. We could have gotten suspended, but Willie let the situation ride. I considered the situation done, but that kicker couldn't stand the fact that I was sitting with a white girl. At that point I knew life in Houston would be a little challenging, too.

Tony was also on the bus. When we got off, he congratulated me for whoopin' that guy. We talked about that for days. Unfortunately, however, the preppies and the valley girls were good friends with this guy. He was some sort of cross between a kicker and a preppie. They didn't appreciate what had happened on the bus, and I knew that there was a plan in place to get me back. Rather than deal with me directly, they began to pick on Tony, which was regrettable because Tony was cool with everyone. His naivete kept him at peace with most of the groups at school. That was one thing I did admire about him.

Eventually, though, they pressed him too much, and Tony and I made a pact to whip some butt. He beat one guy up after school for calling him names and for pushing him around in the lunchroom. After that he wasn't messed with much at all. It was sad that we both had to resort to violence before we got any respect. Even then trouble didn't stop. Someone was always trying one of us. We maintained ourselves and looked out for each other daily. That tension at school only strengthened our relationship.

It became apparent to me that if we were ever going to get our own apartment, my mom was going have to find a good job. We shared a room again while living with my Aunt Ann. Mom had a twin bed, and so did I. This time things were a little better because I was allowed to have a cat. I named him Silver, and he became my little buddy. I never knew how close a person could be to an animal, but that cat got me through many a day.

Now that we lived in the city my mother was able to catch the bus to her job interviews. She couldn't count on Ann much anymore because Ann was so moody. Sometimes she would take Mom to her interviews; sometimes she wouldn't. This made it hard for her because it was rough getting around Houston without being familiar with it. The hot, humid weather didn't help matters much, either.

I remember her getting up early in the morning to search the want ads in the daily newspaper. When she found a prospect she dressed up as best she could and walked in the hot Texas sun to catch a bus. Before she would get to the bus stop she would be sweating. It really hurt me watching her get out there like that, but many times that was the only way she could get to appointments and interviews. She became real frustrated sometimes, but she never gave up. All she needed was a chance, and a chance is what she got.

After several hard months of searching Mom got her first real lead for a good job. Prior to our departure from East Lansing, Mom had been referred to a person who was currently working in the mental health profession in Houston. It took a while, but she finally met this person at a conference. It was then that our lives began to change.

Shortly after the conference, Mom was offered a job at a hospital. What a wonderful day in our lives. The perseverance and hard work paid off. Mom finally got her chance to make it in the professional world. After starting her new job at Riverside General Hospital, we were able to move out of my aunt's apartment. For the first time in almost six months I felt good about the future. We moved into a very nice apartment far away from my aunt on Westheimer. I missed my friends, especially Tony, but I was ready for a change.

After living several places in Houston, Mom and I finally found a community where we wanted to settle down: Spring, Texas, a suburb of Houston. This was the same community my Aunt Linda lived in. For some reason, Spring was the first place Mom and I both felt safe and comfortable since our leaving East Lansing. We moved into a brand new apartment complex too, which, unlike Westheimer, was well kept. The grounds were professionally manicured, and the management maintained a high standard of excellence. This was obvious from the moment we were interviewed by the management staff. Mom and I were very impressed. My only complaint was that the complex had no basketball courts. So I searched one out until I found one at a neighboring apartment complex.

This apartment was better equipped than any place Mom and I had ever lived. It had a vaulted ceiling and a ceiling fan in every room. We had a sizeable kitchen with a dishwasher, garbage compactor, and breakfast nook. Adjacent to the kitchen was a dining room that led out to a spacious patio. The best part was the bedrooms—two of them in this apartment. I was diggin' this because I would finally have my own room again.

My room was the bomb. It included my own bathroom, with an enclosed glass shower and a big two-door closet. It felt like heaven. Peace on earth it was to me. No more bickering or fighting with relatives. No more sharing a room with my mother. I loved my mother—don't get me wrong—but I was embarking on high school, and having my own space was absolutely necessary. The only thing that was left for me to do was to find out about my new school—and to make the basketball team.

Basketball had been a sport that I had always enjoyed. It was the one thing that calmed my soul. When I was on the court, I was completely in charge of my body and mind. The moves I made, the shots I

took, the length of time I played was all up to me. I practiced and practiced the entire summer before school started. I committed myself to
rigorous training and competition. I was determined to make the basketball team at Spring High School. It seemed that my life depended
on it, if I were to make it successfully through high school.

The first day of school arrived, and I couldn't wait to get there. I got
up earlier than usual, dressed, grabbed a bagel topped with honey,
and walked out of the door, greeted by humid air and the sun breaking
through the hazy morning fog. I knew the day was going to be great.
At the bus stop I met a few new neighbors and waited patiently for my
bus. My mother had pre-registered me earlier in the summer, so upon
my arrival at school, all I had to do was report to my homeroom.
When the bus arrived at Spring High, I immediately began looking for
more familiar faces, particularly my cousin Dee, Aunt Linda's son, and
his friends around the way.

This was the first time Dee and I had ever attended a school
together, so I knew it was going to be all that. Dee was always compet-
itive, especially about basketball. He had a hoop in his front yard, and
when I visited he wanted to take me to the court. I usually beat him
pretty bad. After a while, he began to improve his game, and the beat-
ings turned to good competition. However, I still beat him. I never let
him know it, but I was beginning to worry that he would beat me one
day. As I approached the school, there was Dee walking in the hallway.
I spotted him after hearing him laugh his very distinctive laugh. We
talked until the bell rang; then we left each other to attend our first day
of classes. That first day was a good day. The school seemed a wonderful place to be.

The one negative aspect about Spring was that it was a predominantly white school. The suburban white culture was dominant, and
the enrollment at school confirmed that fact. This became more and
more of a problem to me, having to relate to the suburban white community more than to the black community. As I began to be attracted
to girls, I was very reserved because there were few black girls who
attended our school. Rather than spend my time finding a girl friend, I

merely put all my efforts into basketball. It was my hope for the future, I thought

From the beginning of school until mid-fall, through football season, I practiced my basketball game daily. Sports was big around the school. Parents and the community packed the house during the football and basketball games. This excitement from the community poured into the school. It seemed everyone talked about sports, even the bookworms. I knew that my day would come, where the crowds would be cheering my name as I scored points and put on my show. This is what made me so anxious for our tryouts. My chance would come, but it wouldn't be easy.

The day finally came for the basketball tryouts. I reported to the gym with my basketball attire, ready for whatever was about to happen. A herd of running bulls couldn't have kept me away from this opportunity. I was surprised by some of the people who tried out for the team—some were horrible, others were pretty good. The only thing that mattered to me was my making the team.

Soon the tryouts were over, and the coach called all the players into the gym. This was the junior varsity team. I knew if I made the J.V. team, it wouldn't be long before I would be placed on the varsity team. Everything I was dreaming for was riding on the decision of one person, the head basketball coach.

The coaches lined us up vertical to the free throw line. The head coach then began his speech on how impressed he was with each player. Then the bomb was dropped: he said that they couldn't take every player. Some would be left out in the process of picking the new squad for the Spring High School basketball team. He told us he would walk down the line and point to the people who didn't make the team.

He started at the beginning of the line; I was almost at the end. The suspense of the moment was so intense, and my heart was beating so fast that I thought I would pass out. He pointed to the first boy, who, disappointed and ashamed, held his head down and sluggishly walked out of the gym. The coach then walked a little slower down the line and paused for a while like he was confused, then swiftly pointed to the next few people. I could tell that their worlds had been crushed. I began thinking, "What will I do if he points to me?" All of my dreams and hard work over the summer would have been for naught. Although I knew different than that, it would have been hard to see it any other way. Then the coach walked directly in front of me and looked me in my eyes. He pointed to several guys around me, and they left the gym, too. When I turned away from looking at him there were ten people standing on the floor, and I knew I had made the team. "You are the new Spring High School junior varsity team. Your uniforms and shoes can be picked up in the locker rooms. Congratulations fellas," he exclaimed. I was elated. All of my hard worked had finally paid off. I walked with my head up and my chest out for weeks. Spring was the bomb, and was glad to be there.

Within a few weeks of this awesome moment, my mother was informed by relatives in Flint that my grandmother had passed away. Mom was crushed. We flew back to Flint for a couple days to deal with the funeral. While we were there, I remember Mom talking about how awful my grandfather was doing with his alcoholism; it was quickly killing him. I knew that Mom was concerned, but I had no idea that she was considering moving back to Flint.

After we returned to Spring from Flint, Mom was very preoccupied with thoughts about my grandfather. I felt something horrible was about to happen, but I kept my head in the sand. Soon, my mother announced to me that we were moving back to Flint to help my grandfather. The basketball team hadn't even gotten into full season yet. I was in the starting line up, and now I had to give it all up. I felt betrayed, stomped on, and totally disappointed. After all the hard work, sweat and anxiety, I had to leave the basketball team. The one thing that went right was going wrong. It was like a rug being pulled from right under my feet. My grandfather's alcoholism and my mother's heroism were crushing my dreams. I wanted to give up on my family. Once again my mother's life and mine would be in their hands. I couldn't understand it. After all that had happened in our family, my mother was going back to that mess again.

I quit the team, and signed out of the best school I had attended since leaving East Lansing. I knew chaos was before us. I didn't know how it was going to look, but I knew things were going to change again. I wanted to stay in Texas so much, but Mom was set on Michigan. I accepted the decision as best I could, but I didn't like it. As a matter of fact, I hated it and resented my family and my grandfather. It was too hard to be mad at my mother because I knew she just wanted to help, but that was the one thing that often seemed to get us in trouble.

PART FOUR

Identity Crisis

Chapter 14

"...they look upon me as an alien." Job 19:15

Flint: The Return

As much as I hated moving back to Flint, I knew that my mother was not doing it out of malice toward me. Although I was hurt, I knew my grandfather needed help. The only problem was that my mother felt she was the only one who could help. One thing I learned from him and others in my family is that people cannot be helped unless they want to be helped. Granddaddy made it clear that he wanted no help.

This time we didn't fly. Due to finances, we chose to drive back to Flint. It was a boring drive. I guess it took us about a day to get there, Mom driving our used Mustang on the open road. I was really surprised that we made it.

When we arrived, we pulled up to Ann's house, which was on the south side of Flint—not too far from my grandfather's house. Ann had moved back to Flint from Texas shortly before our return. It seemed to me that moving in with her was a bad deal. This would be the second time that I lived with her. Nothing had changed, and I expected the worst.

It didn't take long for us to find out that my intuition was accurate. Ann started tripping right away. We argued constantly, and as each day passed I found more and more creative ways to come home later.

It was best that I stayed away from her because we didn't get along. I never did understand why she was so antagonistic toward me. The whole situation was crazy.

We arrived in Flint during the winter of 1984. The basketball season hadn't started yet, so I knew I would have a chance to join the basketball team. When I found out that I would be attending Flint Central High School, I called the coach immediately. Unfortunately, the school had completed the try-outs, but the coach allowed me to walk on the team after a trial practice. Once again, basketball became my outlet to deal with my personal problems at home. I stayed at school and the gym as much as I could, determined to avoid being around Ann or my grandfather.

That school year was probably the most difficult transition of my life. First of all, I had just gotten used to Spring. I had worked so hard to get on the basketball team, and now having to start all over again was just too overwhelming. Second, the fact that we were living with Ann was traumatic. Over and over again, she mistreated us. Mom never seemed to get the hint that Ann was not a good person to live with. Third, I didn't have my own room. To a teenager in high school, space is very important. I went from having my own room in Spring, Texas, to sharing a room with my mother again in Flint, Michigan. I absolutely hated it. I wondered when we were going to be stable and have our own home; moving so much was quite frustrating. I was hoping that we would soon find a place of our own to settle down.

Unfortunately, things got worse. After experiencing a very antagonistic relationship with Ann, Mom and I moved to my alcoholic grandfather's house. He was the reason we moved back to Flint in the first place. Living with him was worse than living with Ann, so we moved again, to my step uncle's house. That didn't work out either. In three months, we had moved three times. During all of this erratic moving, I was still attending Central and playing basketball. It was a rough time. By the time spring rolled around, Mom had found a small house to rent on the north end of town. She had just found a job, and we were able to finally move out on our own again. Rather than complaining, I maintained and learned to cope with the situation, as usual.

Life really improved after moving to that little house. Mom's experience at the hospital in Houston and her college education turned out to be real assets. I couldn't imagine how she and I would have made it without her college education. Now that we were in Flint, I was determined to make the best of it. The only dilemma was how I was going to fit into the new culture. I had attended suburban white schools most of my life. Now, I was attending a predominantly black high school. Everything was different, from the music to the fashion.

I never realized how different I was from my black peers until I got to Flint Central High School. It was a shock and a wake up call all at the same time. I was a sophomore when we moved back to Flint, and I was a small guy. Had it not been for basketball, I wouldn't have had any social life. It was the first time since attending Dewey Elementary that I had ever been at a predominantly black school. At Spring High School my chances to date black girls were limited, but at Central they were limitless. It almost scared me to death. There were plenty of girls I wanted to approach, but I found that I was insecure and very shy. It didn't help that I had to learn a new fashion and language. Even at an all-black school, I felt completely out of place. The color of my skin was the only thing that kept me in the shadows of reality. Ironically, my skin color made me different at the white schools, so I stood out in them with a special identity, but I was only a number in this black school.

One day after practice, it became extremely apparent that I was out of place when one of the varsity players walked next to me while the other players were in the gym hallway. He was a well-dressed brother, and very popular. As he approached me, he leaned down and motioned for me to move closer to him to hear what he had to say. Then he whispered, "Young brother, you need to put on some socks. You don't live in Texas anymore." I was so embarrassed. I wanted to crawl under a rock, but I played it off as best I could. As he walked away, I just stared out of the window until my ride came.

In addition to that ridicule was the awful nagging of a particular cheerleader who made it known to everyone that I was the new boy on the block. Thanks to her, my name was changed from Nevlynn to "Newboy." Eventually, it seemed that the entire cheerleading squad was calling me "Newboy." She was very cute, but due to my insecurity I couldn't tell if she liked me or if she was merely mocking me. As a result of my shyness, I never confronted her or any of the cheerleaders about this most annoying "Newboy" chant. I figured if I smiled and returned a gesture of friendliness that I would gain a few friends. To my surprise, it didn't work. I simply accepted my new name as a part of being initiated into Flint Central High School.

Really, I hadn't even thought about my dress or my name until these incidents occurred. Not only was I going through changes at the crib, but now I was faced with an identity crisis. The mention of my socks and the mocking of my name were merely a microcosm of what was happening to me on the inside. That brother was right. I didn't live in Texas anymore, but that life was the only life I knew. As much as I hated many of the country hicks and the white rock culture, I wasn't completely adapted to a black culture either. It seemed as though I were an outcast, and that produced a horrible feeling. I think that many blacks deal with this same issue today of being black, but not fitting in with either the black or white communities. I was at a crossroads, and I knew something had to happen. Fortunately, I was only in school for a semester before the school year ended. The summer afforded me time to get myself together, and I was determined to come back a new person.

As the summer approached, I began to develop a strong relationship with my cousin Shawn. She was extremely popular, and every guy in town wanted to hook up with her. Usually grown men would try to talk to her, but she would only flirt with them. We had gotten together and developed a plan to get me in style for the next year, so I went over to her house almost every day. That summer my life revolved around Shawn and basketball. As I met new people and watched the Flint scene, I was able to adapt a bit better. I saved my money from my summer jobs so I could buy all the right clothes. I also played basketball a lot to stay in shape. The funny thing was that in Flint the competition was different.

I learned real quick that the style of basketball that I learned at Spring was not the same style that the brothas had in Flint. The game of basketball in the black community was one of showmanship and strategy. In the white community, it was purely strategy. In Flint the game was more exhilarating and fun with my new peers. They were doing things with the rock that I had never seen at Spring. As a matter of fact, many of the eighth graders in Flint were already dunking by the time they started high school. The white boys in Texas couldn't jump a lick. Much of our team in Texas relied on three point shots and free throws. I felt pretty confident about my abilities in Spring, but in Flint I began to doubt myself. These guys were really good, but the one thing I had a lot of was perseverance. That alone separated me from the masses.

During that summer I also let my hair grow long, almost into an Afro. Shawn convinced me that Gherri Curls were in style and that the popular guys had them. So I allowed Shawn to braid my hair to help it grow even more. Two weeks before the new school year I was ready to get my first perm. It was awfully confusing to me because I ran from wanting to be white, and now I was getting a perm to have straight hair. It was a real paradox, but it seemed to work at the time.

Now that I look back on it, I can't help but wonder if I was more black in Spring, where I was very secure with my hair and my attire. I was attracted to black girls, but there were none. In Spring, I had developed a number of black friends who were raised in middle class families, but I had never thought about getting a curl. Regardless, the Gherri Curl worked in Flint. Immediately, girls who never paid attention to me before began to check me out. My ego was quickly boosted and I think many people, including Shawn, noticed the new confidence that I had.

I also managed to save enough money that summer to buy a car, so I was driving to school during my junior year. It seemed everything was going right. I was about to hit Flint Central in a big new way. It also helped that I grew over three plus inches during the summer and into the fall. I left school before the summer measuring 5'8" and came back in the fall around 6'.

By the time school started I had the new clothes, the new talk, and a new walk. The cheerleader who called me "Newboy" even began to call me by my first name. Within a few weeks of the first day of school, I was ushered into the hall of popularity. I couldn't believe it! Actually, I believe that my confidence was what made a difference. I began to feel all right about myself, and I guess others felt more comfortable with someone who acted and looked like them.

Mine was the basic teenage life: trying to fit in and avoid looking like a fool. I did my best to fit in, but somehow I never felt I truly belonged. It was all about image, and living up to the high school image of popularity was not an easy thing. This was the time in my life when I most wished my father was around because I really needed a man to talk to. If I had to pick a word to sum up my high school teenage years it would be, "Respect."

Chapter 15

"A fool gives full vent to his anger, but a wise man keeps himself under control." Proverbs 29:11

Throw down

Fitting in at Central High school was hard enough without my peers continually bashing me. Prior to my cultural assimilation as a junior, I felt that I had no hope of fitting in. Even with basketball, I still had so many social challenges. There were many times I wished that I could simply disappear.

I managed with a little effort to develop a couple of friendships on the basketball team—my source of credibility. Though I was not the best ball player in the school, I did have a lot of discipline, which set me apart in the fierce competition between my peers. The other fellas around school had a lot of talent, but many of them fell apart when faced with structure and opposition. I admit wholeheartedly that there were several fellas at the school who could have taken my place on the team easily, but I wanted it more than they did.

"How did that brotha get on team? I am way better than he is," my critics would say. I never denied that they were. It seemed to frustrate them that I was there and they weren't, so it seemed that every day someone wanted to try me on the court. At other times, there were even a few folk that wanted to actually fight me, to prove something to themselves. Because I had moved to Flint during the late fall, I had missed the regular try-out. When I got to Flint I called the coach and talked him into allowing me to attend a practice. When he saw me play, he asked me to join the team. A lot of guys really hated that.

So here I was on a basketball team, but still very lost in the crowd at Central. This is when my two homeboys came into play—Slim and Stevie. Slim was a tall, lanky brother who could scratch his knees without bending. He really enjoyed life and, like me, he had a passion for basketball.

Slim and I hung out a lot, and he introduced me to quite a few people. I still couldn't quite seem to find my place, though. After several interludes with a few rough necked brothas and sistas, I decided to limit my acquaintances to Slim and a few other people. Stevie, an Italian guy and one of only two white guys on the team, was one of them. Stevie and I were cool, probably because we sat on the bench together. Yep, we were called the bench warmers, which I hated, but at least I was on the team. So, Slim, Stevie, and I were pretty cool for a while.

My home life really sucked. We still lived with my aunt, and in and out of my grandfather's house. Day after day I would deal with my grandfather's intimidation tactics and my aunt's taunting. I was embarrassed to bring anyone to the house because I just didn't know what was going to happen from one minute to the next. Not only did I not bring anyone home, but I purposely stayed late at the library until bedtime so I could run into the house and go straight to bed. It got to the point that I didn't want to speak to anyone in the house except my mom.

Life was truly hell. I mean it. Had anyone said to me that my situation could have been worse, I would have laughed at them. I was completely miserable. Basketball was my only social outlet. Actually, it was the only emotional outlet for me too. I don't know what I would have done had it not been for basketball.

I didn't realize how much anger had built up inside of me until one day after a rough practice. Usually after practice the team would go to the locker room to get dressed and then would hang out with the cheerleaders in the hallway outside of the gymnasium. As I stood there minding my business, a cheerleader walked up to me to talk. This was not the cheerleader who had badgered me earlier. This young lady was cool and definitely in the minority from my perspective. No girl had approached me at all, and here was a cheerleader talking to me.

"Hey, how ya doin'?" she asked.

"Who, me?"

"Yes, you. How are you?"

"I'm fine, I guess."

"Well, I saw you over here by yourself, and I know you are new here. You moved from Texas, right?"

I could have floated to the clouds. I couldn't believe this girl knew anything about me. I quickly replied, "Yeah, I'm from Texas, but I was born here."

"By the way, my name is Karyn, and you are Nevalyn, right?"

Well, it was close enough. I didn't even have the courage to correct her. I was happy enough that she got most of my name right. As I was about to respond, we were interrupted by one of my team mates.

"Hey, Newboy." I just know you ain't talkin' to my girl."

"Smoke, we're just talkin'," Karyn replied.

"That's all you better be doing. Ain't that right, little man?" Then placing his hand on my head, he smirked, as if he was really going to get away with humiliating me in front of all the cheerleaders and the basketball team.

Had it been a different time and different place I probably would have walked away from that situation. But with all the humiliation, taunting, and frustration that was going on at home, Smoke became the target of my emotional cleansing. Without his knowing it that day, Smoke just happened to be the right person for the wrong reasons. His comments and gestures were condescending. It was just the straw that broke the camel's back.

"Don't touch my head partna'," I replied with anger in my voice.

"What, you getting mad, boy? You betta step before you get your little a _ _ whooped."

"All I have is time," I replied while the entire cheerleading squad and the basketball team watched in amazement.

As I was speaking my peace, I was visualizing how I was going to take him down. Logically, it really didn't look like a contest because he was taller and heavier than I. If I had bet on the fight that day, my wager would have been placed on Smoke. His name was even intimidating. But anger overruled reason and fear, and I could see it all. I was ready for him.

"Well then, lets go little nigga. Let me take my coat off."

I have never understood why people feel like they have a special privilege of undressing before a fight. I have seen this many times. It just doesn't make sense. Why would you give anyone the opportunity to whoop you? I was shorter, lighter, and without question the underdog. I took my window of opportunity while I could. As soon as he began to remove his arms from his coat I lit into him like a bulldog. I mean, I really stuck it to him.

It was on, and I was taking no prisoners. Smoke was going down for the count. I threw blows to his face several times with my fist, and I gave him a few body blows. Every punch that I landed was for all of the humiliating and frustrating times that I had experienced since moving back to Flint. I was angry, and the more I plowed into Smoke the angrier I became.

"This is for me havin' to come back to this place."

"This is for me not fitting in."

"This is for the times I put up with my grandfather's mess."

On and on I must have gone. Everything that was in me was coming out on Smoke. I had no idea that much anger was in my soul.

"Hey little man, get off of him!" shouted one of the team members.

"Somebody grab "Nev!" someone else insisted. Several people from the team pulled me off of Smoke and dragged me to another room outside of the hallway.

"Man, are you crazy? You trying to kill him or something?"

"Nah. He started this. I'm gonna finish it." I said.

"Think about the team man. If coach catches you fighting, then you could get kicked off the team," cried my team mates.

In a funny way, it was the first time I actually felt cared for. They had my best interest at heart. I had just hit that zone though, and I wanted to take Smoke down.

"Go on. Let that little nigga go. He sucka punched me! He sucka punched me! Now Ima kick his little a _ _ !"

"Smoke, let it go," team members pleaded with him. They were trying to hold him back, and trying to keep me out of his sight, but it seemed it was inevitable that this rumble would continue. This was a sho' nuff throw down.

"It's cool y'all. You can let me go," I half-heartedly promised.

"If we let you go, promise you won't do anything. Just walk away."

I wanted to listen to them, but my blood was pumping, and I wanted to finish what I had started. Somehow I persuaded the team to let me go. As I left their arms and turned the corner to go to the hallway, I heard Smoke's voice again. Everyone knew what time it was. No one was holding me down, and no one was holding Smoke down. As I turned the corner our eyes met, and we charged each other like two rams.

Somehow I was able to flip him on the ground. I jumped on him immediately to balance my weight on his upper body, and I let loose on him again. This time I was aiming at his face only. Without notice, I jumped up and dragged him out into the cold evening and grabbed his face and pushed it in the snow over and over again. I wanted to see Smoke bleed and suffer. I wanted him to hurt and be humiliated the way he had humiliated me. Had it not been for Slim, I would have killed him. I know it because Smoke wasn't even a factor anymore; he was just a representative for the pain I was feeling, and I was determined to kill that pain. Luckily, Slim pulled me off of him.

After that fight I got much respect from a lot of people. The word around school was that the new boy whooped the heck out of Smoke. No one could really believe it, nor could I. For weeks and even months after that event, Smoke would be plagued by the fact that I had embarrassed and whooped him. I remembered my uncle's advice to me so many years ago when I was afraid of the school bully: beat the toughest guy and the others will leave you alone. Well, that's what happened. I had a few confrontations after that, but nothing major like what happened to Smoke and me that day.

Reflecting on that incident, I can now understand how a boy can explode and take someone else's life. Many at-risk teens live with frustrations, fear, disappointments, and varying degrees of anger every day. It just takes one minute to leave the world of sanity and enter the world of insanity.

Once again, I do believe that the Lord, through Slim, had his hands on me that day because I might have killed Smoke—not because I was tougher than he was, nor because I was a thug type—but because I was simply frustrated and angry. Smoke just happened to be my outlet.

Chapter 16

"Many waters cannot quench love; neither can the floods drown it."

Song of Solomon 8:7

High School Love

It never really occurred to me that I would fall in love in high school. In fact, due to my shyness, I figured that my relationships would be superficial and quick. By the time I was a junior at Central High there were several girls who were aggressively pursuing me. Usually, I avoided those types, reasoning that if a relationship was going to happen, it would have to be a *mutual pursuit*. I was determined not to make myself look like a fool by pursuing someone who would in turn reject me, so I waited for the right time and place. I was bound to hook up with someone, but I knew for sure that it would have to be at another school. I had a rule about never dating a girl from the same school I attended, an approach that I thought would keep gossip to a minimum.

As a result, I only had two significant relationships in high school, both of which went much deeper than they should have. These two young ladies tied up close to two of my high school years. They had my nose wide open, as the saying goes. If I had to do it all over again, I would have dated more. I needed the experience. Further, high school is a time to enjoy life and have fun. Most teenagers haven't even gotten to know themselves yet, and may not be ready for a serious commitment. But I didn't know this, and I thought my relationships would go the distance.

Of the two serious love affairs, Robin's and mine was the most impacting. I dated her most of my senior year. As far as I was concerned, Robin was the right one for me. I was head over heels for this girl, though I no longer know why. My entire life revolved around Robin and basketball. Sometimes I think she knew that, but I was too gullible at the time to keep the relationship in perspective because I didn't want to lose her.

Robin lived on the north side of Flint and attended Flint Academy, where all the fine girls went. She wasn't the bomb, but she was mature and finessed. Unlike many of the school girls, Robin knew how to present herself without seeming too pushy or desperate. I liked that. She was short, brown-skinned, and shapely—not too skinny and not too big, but just right. She wore a weave, but her own hair was medium length. I think what I really enjoyed about her was her smile. Robin had a smile that made me melt. She was very charming, and I wanted to be with no one else.

I met Robin one day when I was working at a small, part-time job at a clothing store in the mall. I was able to keep in fashion that way. I was getting big discounts on all the clothes. Working at this store also catapulted me into a new social world. I was able to meet a lot of people, especially the girlies.

While I was at work, Robin walked in the store wearing a Ponderosa uniform. Ponderosa was a popular family restaurant. When I looked in her eyes I knew that I was gonna get the digits, but I had to be suave about it. I walked over to her as she was looking at the sweaters. Before I could open my mouth, she began to ask me questions about the sizes and variety of styles of the sweaters in stock. I was glad to help her out. I guess I did a good job, because she left me with her phone number. It was on after that.

Usually, when the fellas met a new honey, it was something to talk about. But one had to be careful sharing information, because there were plenty of player haters. I happened to be pretty tight with two guys who were in my first period typing class. The next day after meeting Robin, I was pumped to get to class to tell my boys about my latest situation. As life goes, I was not really able to get down with the facts right away, because my boy Jay was tripping about this young lady who was dogging him. I swear, I listened to him for about a week before I could even tell him that I had met a girl from the same school that his girl was attending. I felt bad for the brother, because he was really into this girl, but she kept giving him the blues. I couldn't take much more so I told Jay to give her the walking papers.

For a while things seemed to get better for Jay and life was feeling awfully good to me. I was spending a lot of time with Robin, and making money at the clothing store. There was not much else I could ask for. One day in class for some odd reason Jay started bringing up this relationship of his again, but this time he wanted to know more details about my girl. I was so absorbed in the moment that I didn't think twice to indulge the brother. So for the entire class period, Jay and I talked about details about his ex-girlfriend and my new girlfriend. By the time class ended, we were just looking at each other in awe. Jay's ex-girlfriend happened to be Robin.

There was an understood rule between some of the guys at school. If one of us talked to a girl, the others in our group would not. It was just out of respect. This time around things were different, because I honestly never knew that he was hooked up with Robin. He never even mentioned her name during any of our conversations. As a matter of fact, all I remember him talking about was how much he wanted her. Not once did I hear that the feelings were reciprocated. I was struck to make a decision at the end of class that day. I apologized to Jay, but I gave him no more information about my situation with Robin. I completely stopped talking about it. So did he. Jay and I never did speak to each other as much after that.

In the meantime, I had to make some decisions. I went directly home that day and called Robin. I wanted to confront her about this newfound information. When I did, Robin didn't even seem fazed about it. She simply replied that she never liked him. At the time, that was good enough for me. Robin and I never did talk about Jay again. I felt bad for my boy, but it didn't seem right to walk away from Robin when she felt that there was no relationship in the first place. As a result, my friendship with Jay changed. I regretted it a little, but not enough to squash my love thing for Robin.

Robin and I kicked it well for more than half of my senior year. I was always at her house. Her mother loved me and so did her grandmother. I was in like Flinn. She worked right across the street from me at Ponderosa, so I would go over and visit her during my breaks and after work. That girl was forever working, but it didn't matter; it was all good. The more we were together the more I felt right about our relationship. I felt nothing, I mean nothing, could go wrong.

During one of my workdays, Robin came by to visit on her lunch break as usual. This time one of my associates, Silk, from another store was visiting when she came by. Silk, was a career community college student. I don't think he ever graduated with his associates after four years of study.

After her brief visit, Silk asked me about her. I indulged him a little bit, because I was proud of the fact that she was my girl. I never thought once that this college-age brother would be checking out high school girls, but he was. Worst than that she was checking him out. After a while, going into the spring semester I noticed things changing between Robin and me. Suddenly, she didn't want me to come over to her house or drop in at her job. Actually, it wasn't two weeks into the new semester before I was dumped. Yeah, I was dumped and couldn't figure out why. I moped around for days wondering what had happened.

Then one day as I was coming into work, I saw Robin and my college associate hugging intimately in the mall. I was enraged, surprised, angry, and hurt. I felt like a volcano ready to erupt. She turned around and I was just standing there looking. I know I looked like an idiot, because I felt like one. When she saw me she simply turned her head and walked away. Silk tried to play it off by waving to me. I fronted him by saying something mean and abusive. Then I confronted him physically in middle of the mall. I know I looked like an idiot, but my pride was bruised and I wanted reparation at that point.

He walked away and tried his best to avoid me that entire day. I went to work right after that confrontation, but I couldn't get it off my mind. The more I thought about it the angrier I got. Soon, my boss noticed that I was pissed off. I had no focus and my customer service skills were horrible. Frankly I had a bad attitude. What made the whole situation even worse was that Robin was going to the prom with me in just a couple of months. I had lost my girlfriend and my prom date. I was up a tree. That's when my boss, Michelle, tried to console me. She was a local college student her self and I'm telling you she was fine. She offered to go to the prom with me, and assured me that it would be an honor to do so. Had I been thinking at the time, I would have taken her up on it.

At the time I was so infatuated with Robin and the whole prom situation that I turned her down flat. Realizing that I was bad for business for that day, my boss let me off of work. I walked out of the store with my mind made up. I was gonna kill Silk. I felt betrayed and duped. He was going to pay for my felt loss. I drove around Flint for hours looking for him, but I never found him, at least that day. I thank God to this day that I didn't. No telling what would have happened.

Believe it or not, I got over Robin. It took a while, but I did it. Ironically, she ended up going to the prom with me anyway. It was the worst mistake in the world. I would have been better off going by myself.

Jay came back to mind as I was sitting in my room one day. I began to think of his hurt and anguish earlier that year. Had I listened to my mind rather than my heart, this girl would never have hurt me. I vowed from that time on to never get involved with any young lady who had been in a previous relationship with any of my boys. I also vowed to stay away from Flint Academy, because I had been in two horrible relationships with two girls from the same school. DeShonne was the other person that broke my heart, but she and I had not dated as long as Robin and I. Two was enough, so Flint Academy was out of the picture for the rest of the year. I never thought that love could hurt so much, but it did. I got hard after that, but couldn't seem to stay that way. But I did manage to stay out of serious relationships until it was time for me to get out of Flint.

Chapter 17

"…but the income of the wicked brings them punishment."
Proverbs 10:16

Russell Street

In most inner cities I believe that nearly all teenagers come into contact with gangs and drugs, either directly or indirectly. I was directly affected by both. Of course, that a few of my family members were involved with drugs and all types of crime wasn't new to me, but to see it from the high school level was different. I never could align myself with the criminal element. I never desired to take drugs either, so I avoided a lot of trouble while attending high school.

Living in Flint, where it wasn't hard to find trouble, was risky enough. During the mid-eighties, gangs and drugs began to sweep our town, and the police developed crime units that specialized in cracking down on youth crime. As I drove from the south side to the north side, it was more apparent to me how bad things were getting. There seemed to be more gang graffiti and activity on the north side. I did my best to stay clear from it all, but it was hard. As the gang activity increased, so did the popularity of a particular gang the Young Boys Incorporated, or as they called themselves, the YBI's. This group was out of Detroit, but there were a few cliques in Flint. The power of the group became apparent to the entire city one day in the summer of 1987.

On this particular day, Slim and I decided to skip our cafeteria lunch at school and, instead, drive to McDonalds. This was something we often did, and we had never gotten caught. On the way out, we noticed L.P., and we asked him if wanted to go with us, but he had other plans.

Later in the day, just before the last bell, I was standing in the hallway talking with a few of my friends when I saw L.P. walking toward me. "What's up L.P.?" I said, but he walked right past me without speaking. I got an attitude at first. Then I looked a little harder at him and I noticed his affect was off. L.P. looked as if he had seen a ghost. So I figured he was just having a bad day or something.

Apparently, there was a drug house located on Russell Street, and the YBI's had come into town and killed everyone that was in that house—more than eight people, I think. The reason L.P. looked so bothered earlier in school was that he had just left the house. L.P. was notorious for getting high. That entire week was tense for a lot of people because in a small place like Flint, it was common knowledge that this gang was in town. It became more apparent when the Detroit clique came up, caravanning all the way to Flint without being stopped by the police. They drove around in limousines and jeeps, asking people various questions about the house on Russell Street. The word on the street was that someone had escaped the house, and the YBI's were looking for him. I never knew if they found him. I do know someone's money was messed around, which is why the murders occurred in the first place.

That drug world was never something I was drawn to, so when I did go to the north side I stayed clear of Russell Street. I could see the power and influence of gangs and drugs. After that event, I knew several people who wanted to align themselves with a gang or clique for protection. If it wasn't the YBI's, then it was a gang called the Smurfs. I don't know how these guys came up with these names.

Today gangs are epidemic in society. Almost every town in the country has a gang. It is so different than it was years ago, but I guess there are more broken families and more displaced and hopeless kids, so they turn to these gangs, and the drugs are merely a means to an end.

I am glad that I didn't choose the gang path; I can sleep at night knowing that I have done my neighbor right. Many of these brothers and sisters can't feel that. Running and looking behind your back becomes a lifestyle. Looking at a few members in my family had already helped me to draw that conclusion. The thug life just wasn't worth it then, and it is not worth it now.

Chapter 18

"Oh, that I had the wings of a dove! I would fly away..." Psalm 55:6

Graduation

In high school I used to think that my future was relatively well planned. After high school graduation, I always believed that I would go immediately to college. At the time, Michigan State University was my college of choice, located in East Lansing, a place of fond memories to which I always wanted to return. I planned to pursue a career in electrical engineering or architecture, believing that a successful professional life was definitely ahead of me. I had no doubt that my future would be any different until one day after school when Slim and I were at his house discussing our graduation and future plans.

With confidence he told me that he was going to the military; with uncertainty I said that I wanted to attend Michigan State University. Slim's response took me by surprise:

"Man, you don't want your mother paying for college. Can she even afford it?"

By that time, Mom had gotten a position as a therapist, working for a major consulting firm in Flint. Moms was making bank! She was successful and could afford my college education, but all of a sudden I began to think about the connection I would have with my mom. The cost of college was not the issue: my independence was at stake. In the few short moments of my conversation with Slim, I realized that the military could be my ticket to independence, and he and I began talking about going in together. Since I knew my mother would be totally disappointed, I avoided discussing it with her until I was sure that I had been accepted.

Slim and I were told by one of his brothers that the best branch of the military to enter was the air force. Within a few days, Slim and I went up to visit the air force recruiter. I was sure that I wasn't going to any other branch. If the air force turned me down, I was going directly to college. When we arrived at the recruiting office, two sharply dressed women approached us and told us that we would have to pass a test before they could begin to talk to us about military career options. Even though I hated tests, I figured I could score high enough to get into the air force. We were to take the test immediately. I passed it the first time, but Slim never did, so I ended up being the lone ranger. Slim decided to enlist in the army. I was disappointed that my boy wasn't going with me, but I was excited about my new future.

For several months, Slim and I discussed our plans with our other friends at school. Some thought we were crazy; others thought it was kind of cool. Ultimately, their thoughts didn't matter. I had to be sure of my decisions for myself. Some of my teachers thought it would be best for me to attend college right out of high school, but I wanted my independence so much that my ears were closed to anything they had to say. Everyone knew about my decision except my mother. I hadn't signed any papers because I hadn't turned eighteen yet. My mother had to sign me over to the military, and I knew she wasn't going for that. Just thinking about telling Mom about my decision to go to the military was intimidating.

She was doing very well as a successful therapist in Flint, and we were able to move to the suburbs. We lived in the city of Grand Blanc, a most beautiful and peaceful community. It was there that I took the chance of telling my mother about my decision to go to the air force. If there had been any way for me to avoid talking to her about it, I would have taken it. I waited for her to come home from work to tell her.

When she got home, we had the usual greeting, then I went straight for the blow.

"Mom, I need to talk to you about something important."

She sat down on the coach in the living room waiting to hear what I had to say.

"Mom, instead of going to college right away, I'm going to the air force. They will even pay for my education."

She just stared at me for a while, almost like she didn't hear me. Then I began to repeat what I had previously said, but before I could finish she simply replied "No." Of course, we got into a heated argument, but after a while she grew quiet, believing—I think—that I would change my mind. I never did.

For a long time Mom didn't like talking about my future, especially with her friends. I could only imagine what was going on in her mind. Mom's only son was enlisting in the United States military. My real hope was that she would see beyond her immediate fears and support my decision. Unfortunately, that didn't happen until I was actually in the military.

The reality hit my mother when she had to sign the paperwork to release me from her custody. I'll never forget that cool, fall day. I went to the recruiter's office after school to fill out paper work for my mother to sign. From there, the recruiter and I drove to my mother's office, which was on the second floor of a prominent, downtown building. Her window faced the street, making it easy for her to see everyone entering the building. I am sure she saw us, which probably put her in a bad mood.

The recruiter and I walked in. I spoke to Mom's secretary, then we went straight to her office. Her door was wide open. She was ready for us. I introduced the recruiter to my mother, and Mom reluctantly shook her hand. We sat down on a couch, which faced Mom's desk. She squared up in her chair, more serious than I had ever seen her before. The recruiter wasted no time.

"Ms. Johnson, we are here, as you know, for you to sign the authorization papers for Nevlynn's air force enlistment. Your permission and signature will release your son to our custody."

Mom looked at me, and I looked at the recruiter. Mom was silent for an uncomfortable, eternal minute. Then she said to me, "Tubby, are you sure this is what you want to do?" When I nodded yes, she reached out to take the paperwork, and in less than five minutes, the transaction was completed. She handed the signed documents to the recruiter, stood up, and walked us out of her office.

"Tubby, I'll see you later," Mom said.

I felt independent right away. I was leaving Flint and all the bad memories that went with it. The recruiter didn't say much on the way back to the office. It was almost as if she understood. After all, my recruiter was a mother too. When we got back, I was given a date for a physical. Things went relatively smooth after that. I was now a military man. Mom didn't want to sign the papers, but I think she realized that I was old enough to make my own decisions. As much as it hurt her, she gave me an opportunity to decide my own course in life.

That school year ended quick, and Slim left for army basic training right after graduation, but it was a long and boring three summer months before I was able to get out of Dodge. Watching all of my friends leave for college was hard. The girl who called me "Newboy" during my sophomore year went to Spelman. Several of my other friends went to local colleges and universities, Michigan State being one. I envied every one of them just a little. As a matter of fact, I truly began to wonder if I had made the right decision. I was dating a young lady a little bit during the summer of my senior year, and I was really diggin' her, too. She was the only girl I was ever scared to kiss. Anyway, she was headed for Michigan State University. Once the school year started, I visited her and a few of my friends there, but I didn't feel like I really belonged. So I maintained, and I followed my initial plan to pursue the military.

The date finally came—October 1987—and I was ready to get the heck out of Flint. My bags were all packed, but I had to wait for Mom to get home to drive me to the bus station. I know she was hoping that I had changed my mind, but I hadn't; I was set on this course with no thought of turning back. She walked in the house, and I hugged her. Then without any words, I picked up my luggage and headed straight for the car. Mom followed unwillingly behind me, and we quietly rode to the bus station. I didn't know what to say.

By the time we got to the Greyhound Station, I was ready to get out and board the bus because I didn't want to deal with the crying, but the bus hadn't arrived yet, so Mom and I waited and engaged in small talk until it came. Then we stood outside to wait for all the people to get off the bus. Up to that point, I don't remember Mom saying anything to me about my decision. She did tell me that if the military people mistreated me that I would always be able to come back home. I appreciated her words of love, but I was determined to make it, and she knew it. Soon the bus was empty, and I was able to board. I turned around and hugged Mom. She hugged me back, not seeming to want to let go. At that moment it hit me that I was actually leaving her for the first time in my life. I had dreamed of the day I would leave Flint and the Johnson family for as long as I could remember, but I never realized that it would be such a sad occasion for Mom and me. When she finally released me, I turned and quickly boarded the bus. I sat down by a window, so I could get a last look at everything. Mom stood outside staring at the bus and looking very alone and afraid. I knew she wanted to be happy for me, but it was hard for her. As the bus doors closed, I watched her wave to me; then she walked towards her car. I could see that she was crying. That hurt, because I never wanted to be the reason that my mother cried.

To my surprise, tears began to flow from my eyes. This woman that I watched walking to her car had overcome so many obstacles in life. She was able to break away from a dysfunctional family, overcome hurdle after hurdle, pursue an education, and succeed in college. This same woman raised a son without the help of a man. Though her family abused her and mocked her, she was still able to forgive them and help them—sometimes out of a need to be needed—but she was there for many of them, anyhow. The woman that I watched walking back to her car was a strong black woman who, by default, took the place of a man in many respects. I knew then how much I really loved her. I would give my life for my mother because I knew she had already given her life for me. Mom made a lot of mistakes, and made choices that put both of our lives in jeopardy, but I know without a shadow of a doubt that God made a way. So I cried in that window seat, knowing that Mom was crying too. I would miss my mother dearly, but I knew it was time for me to find my way in life.

PART FIVE

The Real World

Chapter 19

"As iron sharpens iron, so one man sharpens another."
Proverbs 27:17

Reality Check

Before heading to basic training, I had to process the Detroit Metro Processing Station where the atmosphere was cold and sterile. Several hundred recruits like me were in various lines awaiting physicals and interviews. The experience was rather intimidating. In addition, I noticed that the military personnel treated me differently depending on their respective roles. For example, it seemed that my recruiter had cared for me as a person as opposed to these processors, who were acting as though I were only a number. As I was being shuffled around I thought to myself that I had beaten the odds. I was living and doing something positive with my life, so as intimidating as this experience was, I wasn't going to allow this short experience to break me down. I was determined to make it, no matter what. I had come to far to turn back now.

As soon as I entered the building, the commands started. "Go here!" "Sit there!" "Jump!" "Stand!" It was a continuous and horrible onslaught against my ego and pride. Between the commands and the constant moving, I was barely able to catch a breath and sit down. But when I did, I was shocked to see Mike, one of the kids I had grown up with in East Lansing. He was taller, his hair was hot red, and he was

117

much broader, but I knew it was Mike, though it had been almost six or seven years since I had seen him. Although we hadn't been the best of friends, it was good right then to see a familiar face. I headed toward him to say hello before the dictators returned. When I approached, Mike looked up and seemed just as shocked as I was.

"Hey! Nevlynn, right?" He said.

"Yeah, it's me, Mike. How's life going for you?"

We spent the next half hour catching up. Mike was going to the army to become a "grunt," a trained legal assassin. He proudly admitted that he wanted to get in and kill some folk. I thought to myself, "How ludicrous. Who would really want to kill someone?" Mike had grown mean and bitter, and his meanness was pouring out like acid. It was unfortunate that he had no other plans than to join the military to kill folks, but that seemed to fit him. Mike had been a gung-ho, GI type even when we were in East Lansing. Now he would be a certified killer. Scary thought! I never saw him after the dictators in green returned and we had to split up.

Around 4:00 p.m. all of the Air Force recruits were escorted to a hotel that was in bad shape. The place had no charm, no allure. It was simply a building with rooms. I felt like a test rat. When I entered my room, I knew the honeymoon period was over. I was moving closer and closer to reality.

Lying on my bed, I began to question my choice. Had I made the right decision? My brain was cooking with afterthoughts of yesterday and boiling with the urgency to know what tomorrow would bring. As my mind filled with these thoughts, someone walked into the bedroom. I jumped up in shock because I wasn't expecting company. Luckily, this unexpected person turned out to be my roommate. Our processors called all the recruits by their last name, so we did the same. My roommate simply introduced himself as Cates. Cates was a medium height, bright-skinned brother with a lot of personality. He was from Detroit, and knew the streets well. Cates and I immediately began to discuss our decision to join the military. While my story was probably typical, his wasn't. Cates, a member of the gang Young Boys

Incorporated, had gotten into some trouble, and the only way he could escape was to leave town. I guess his clique was cool because they let him out without beating him to death. He didn't seem thrilled about the decision, but he was overjoyed by this second chance to get his life together and happy to get out of town alive.

Cates and I worked up a hefty appetite after talking so much, and he offered to take me to Greektown to get a bite to eat. That was cool, I thought, because I wanted to get out of that drab hotel and see something better. Within minutes Cates and I were on the Detroit streets which, unlike Flint's, beat with the pulse of their big, metropolitan city. Everything in Detroit seemed bigger, brighter, and faster. Greektown was a festive, downtown tourist trap with several restaurants and shopping centers, and we hung out at a pizza joint for a short while, enjoying ourselves, but I began to worry about getting back to the hotel on time. It was almost 8:00 p.m., and we had to make it back before the nine-thirty lock down. We got back just as security was about to lock the door.

When I walked into my room I was more tired that I thought. Actually, I was exhausted—not by the night out on the town—but by the full events of the day. A lot was happening, and I don't think I was processing it quickly enough. I took a long shower and began to relax. After putting my night clothes on, I lay in bed, looking up at the ceiling for a while, once again thinking about my life. Soon I was asleep.

Hours later I was awakened by some nut running down the hallway knocking on all of the doors, screaming, "Get up! Everybody get up! It's time to ship out!"

This was crazy. I felt that I hadn't slept very long, and now I was getting up to ship out. I wasn't diggin' this at all, and I couldn't believe how excited and upbeat this guy was, waking people up at five o'clock in the morning. This was an accurate foreshadow of coming events, however. I should have known that life wasn't going to get any easier.

After eating a sloppy helping of what seemed like Dr. Suess' green eggs and ham, all of the recruits were ushered onto a chartered bus destined for the Detroit Airport. It was dark outside, and we were very quiet. Prior to breakfast, we had been given brown envelopes with our names printed on them. "Don't open this envelope, under any circumstances," a hefty sergeant had instructed us. What do you do? You have an envelope with your name on it, but no rights to view its contents. It really bothered me that I couldn't open that envelope, but my respect for authority kept me from doing so.

So there we were, Uncle Sam's boys, standing in the Detroit Airport, looking like lost puppies. It was obvious that our group was unfamiliar with the protocol. We were told to stay in one spot until another military person greeted us. We obeyed. Soon a shapely, white woman with blonde hair approached us wearing a nicely fitted nylon, blue uniform. "Follow me," she said. We obeyed. As far as I knew, we could have been led to slaughter. But that's the thing about the military: superiors don't expect their subordinates to ask questions, but just to do as they're told.

This woman led us to a small room located in the airport. She looked at each of our brown envelopes, gave a short talk, and then gave us instructions for the rest of the day. We recruits were then escorted to the Continental Airlines concourse. Cates and I sat together and rapped about our love lives, which seemed like something to talk about. In reality, we had no love lives; we were simply lust-filled kids, with little vision for the future. More than five hours passed before our group boarded the plane, which upset me because we had been woken up so early. The next stop would be San Antonio, Texas.

When the plane landed, I was excited and anxious to find out what would lie ahead. Another person, this time a man, approached our large group and directed all of us to another chartered bus. By the time we got to San Antonio, it was late at night. The group boarded the bus and off we went into the wild blue yonder. I didn't dare talk, at least not too loudly because everyone was quiet. There seemed to be an unstated understanding there would be no talking. After all, this was a serious situation for most of us. I could feel the tension in the air. Even Cates, the gang banger was serious. These uniformed men had intimidated well over sixty people that they had never met before—an amazing feat. The slow, quiet bus ride lasted almost an hour. All I could do was sit in my seat and look out the window thinking, "What in God's name have I done?"

The road grew darker and more eerie as the bus approached the base. Not spotting a light anywhere, I wondered how that bus driver was able to see the pitch dark road. The engine idled down, and a sign lit by floodlights mysteriously appeared: "Welcome to Lackland Air Force Base." Two military policemen stood several feet from the sign, blocking the entrance to the base. Tall, silver fences with barbed wire on top surrounded this place. I was beginning to see where I was headed. My colleagues and I were entering a twilight zone. This felt like a bad dream, and I immediately became defensive and thought I'd better toughen up psychologically.

"I'm from Flint, and I'm a bad brother," I nervously assured myself. "I can take whatever comes," I strained to believe.

As we approached the gates to the base the military policeman slowed the bus to a stop with one quick motion of the hand. He then directed the bus toward a building with bright lights. I began to think twice about my sorry decision and started doing what I could to pump myself up so I wouldn't freak out. Insecure and on shaky ground, I began to talk to myself again: "Okay man. It's gonna be all right. You can do this, now!"

The bus pulled over at a tall, cement building. Three men wearing round-brimmed hats and looking like state troopers stood in the open doors and greeted us. No one really wanted to get off the bus, but had we not I think we would have been pulled off. The angry looking men who stood waiting for us were T.I.'s, Technical Instructors. I could see that they were mean with attitudes. Maybe they had just eaten a bad dinner or something, I thought, hoping their dispositions were temporary. Whatever the reason, it was clear that they were about to take out their bad day on us. Just then, the bus doors closed, and the driver angled the bus to pull it away from this dreary place. I almost cried. With the bus gone, there would be no way of escape.

Bellowing like thunder, the men in blue began to call every one of us names that I had only heard on the street—and some that I had never heard. These guys were profane, loud, and pissed off at the world. They displayed a mentality that I thought I had left behind in Flint. We recruits were commanded to form a straight line for inspection. Actually, I believe this was a humorous exercise for the T.I.'s, who paraded down the line and took turns insulting each person. One recruit from Cleveland, Ohio, was wearing a long gherri curl. When the T.I. saw his hair, he had a complete field day with that brother. I don't know what he was thinking, leaving home with a gherri curl. I had gotten my head shaved several months prior, not wanting to give anyone in the military the satisfaction of cutting my hair.

For some reason, as the white T.I.'s approached me, I shifted mentally, their hollering and intimidating reminding me of Humble, Texas. Sgt. Link, one of the T.I.'s, stepped right in my face and leaned his big, black-rimmed hat on my nose. Without thinking I drew back to hit him, but Cates stopped me. Had I made the mistake of hitting that man, I wouldn't be writing about this scenario today. I do believe they would have taken me out. After noticing my body movement, the sergeant dared me to flinch, but I didn't. I maintained. Again, I was determined to make it. I wasn't going to let anyone mess up my opportunity, not even a T.I.

After the T.I.'s finished threatening and insulting us, they marched us to our dorms. The dorm room, resembling sets from the mini series M.A.S.H., had row upon row of neatly made beds and tidy lockers, situated on shiny, slick floors surrounded by bright white walls. Everything was green and white in this place and sterile as a surgical needle. We recruits were assigned beds and ordered to go to sleep. As I got into my bed, which was as tight as a rubber sheet, I began thinking about all of my friends at Michigan State University. I envisioned them sitting in their dorm rooms eating pizza and talking about the good old days while I was ordered to go to sleep in an open hall with thirty other guys I didn't know. Two I could deal with. Three I could tolerate, but thirty was absolutely freaky.

I took a deep breath and rolled over on my bed as soon as I could. I had been hesitant about even moving in the bed, afraid I would mess it up. My life was beginning to suck. I wanted out of there right away, but I had made a commitment to myself to graduate, and graduate was what I was determined to do. Eventually, I put myself to sleep by fantasizing that the whole thing was a bad dream. But such fantasies are soon dispelled. I would have to wake up the next day to the cold reality that this was no dream; rather, it was my new life.

The following morning a loud siren accompanied by deafening slams and piercing screaming awakened us. I thought my heart would jump out of my mouth. Not knowing how to respond, I just rolled out of the bed as quickly as I could, jumped to my feet, and assumed the position of attention. My new roommates did the same thing. The mad men had returned, but now they were really pissed off. It was about five in the morning, and the crickets were still sleeping, but we were up and being herded down the stairs to listen to our T.I.'s berate us into shape. I truly believed that Satan had sent these men straight from hell to terrorize us. As a matter of fact, I didn't believe they were men at all for they seemed to have no compassion for us.

The days began to pass by quickly, and our flight learned to be air-men. I thought the name 'airmen' was corny, but that's what we were called. The thirty people who lived in my dorm were called a 'flight.' The squadron consisted of the entire sixty guys, thirty of whom were in another flight class located downstairs from us. My squadron speedily learned how to shine boots, clean floors, fold underwear in three-inch squares, iron, sew, and scrub walls. Of the many things we learned, folding underwear in three-inch squares must have influenced me the most because I still fold my underwear. Within two weeks, I began to see what was happening. I was actually learning how to work with people. That's what this thing was all about: learning to work together with pride and purpose.

After six weeks of intense pressure, I began to like my T.I.'s. They did, indeed, have compassion, but they had to conceal it in order to do their job: training sixty people to function as one unit. In a combat or other tense situation, our squadron would have to think with one brain. Once we airmen understood their purpose the T.I.'s earned much respect from us. They had taken a group of young men and torn down our walls of racism and classism. Slowly, I was beginning to see what we were becoming: a family that would be able to work together as one functioning body. And there was another bonus for me: basic training turned out to be one of the few times in my life when I felt my color was of no particular interest to the ones in charge. Basic training taught me that when people come together for one goal, a lot can be accomplished.

When it was time to graduate after only six short weeks, I was reluctant to leave. I had grown close to my T.I.'s and my squadron brothers. Lackland Air Force Base had permanently changed me. I gained a level of confidence I had never experienced before. Now, I was on to the real military.

Chapter 20

"Why embrace the bosom of another man's wife?"
Proverbs 5:20

Brandy

After basic training, I went directly to technical school in Biloxi, Mississippi, to learn my trade. I stayed there for eight weeks; then I was transferred to my first permanent base, Barksdale Air Force Base in Louisiana. While attending technical school, I was privileged enough to have the resources to purchase my first brand new car. I bought a 1988 Ford EXP, black and gold and drove it to Barksdale from Mississippi. My car was the bomb. What I enjoyed most was that I was free to come and go when I wanted to.

When I arrived at Barksdale, I met Brandy, the finest woman I had ever seen. Brandy had been writing to me through a sponsorship program while I was stationed in Mississippi. New people arriving on base were assigned personal sponsors to help them get acclimated, but when I saw Brandy I was hoping for more than a tour of the base because she was drop dead gorgeous. Up until that day, it would have been hard for anyone to convince me that the military had attractive women. Brandy changed that opinion right away and redefined the sponsorship program for me. I thought to myself, "Every man should be greeted and acclimated to his new environment by a woman like

this." It was a real treat. I was proud that I would have such a beautiful woman as my sponsor for the next few weeks.

Brandy took me to my office and introduced me to my first boss,
Lisa Pardo. The office had been a little behind in work, so I was gladly
welcomed. Lisa ushered me into the 2nd Avionics Maintenance
Squadron and introduced me to everyone in the building. Brandy
asked Lisa if she should wait for me, but Lisa told her no. I wanted to
beg Brandy to stay, but she left.

"I'll call you later. OK?" she said.

I looked in her eyes and nodded with approval. Lisa could tell I had
a major attraction thing going on with Brandy.

"Attractive young lady, huh?" Lisa commented.

"Yes, indeedy!"

That was the end of our conversation about Brandy. For the next
few hours, I was escorted through a high security building—boring
stuff compared to the few minutes I had spent with Brandy. As soon as
my introduction to the squadron was complete, Lisa allowed me to
leave, and I went to the dorm to start unpacking my gear. Brandy
stopped by while I was unpacking.

"How did you know where I would be living?" I asked.

"I'm your sponsor. I know everything," she answered.

For some reason I felt comforted by her confidence. After I
unpacked, Brandy and I set out to get a bite to eat. On the way back
from dinner, Brandy came up to my room with me, and we talked for
a good while. She even helped me unpack a few more items from my
boxes.

As she was getting ready to leave for the night, Brandy asked if I
would go to the movies with her the next night. I agreed quickly. Who
wouldn't have? She closed the door, and I was left in my dorm room
by myself. It was a nice room, with wall-to-wall carpet, brand new oak
furniture, two twin beds, and two wall lockers. I was rather
impressed. I sat on my bed in awe of the events that had happened
that day, but before I could mellow out and indulge in thoughts of my

new sponsor, there was a knock at the door. I got up to answer it, and there stood a young brotha.

"Hey, young blood. Welcome to the war."

Rodney was one of those brothers that knew everything about everyone on base. I stepped out of my room to talk to him, then followed him down the hallway to meet a few of the dorm rats, as he referred to them. There had to be about ten guys hanging out in his room, a few of them playing cards, and others reading magazines, watching TV, or just smoking and drinking. The scene reminded me of Flint in the summertime when people would bring their card tables out to their front yards and get loud and crazy playing cards. It was obvious that black folk were the same in Louisiana as they were in Flint.

"Hey y'all. This is the new brotha on base," said Rodney.

After everyone greeted me Rodney took me to the side and congratulated me on keeping company with Brandy. As it turns out, Brandy was well sought after by the fellas on base, but she was married. According to Rodney, her husband treated her badly and messed around on her with other women.

I stood in the room for a few moments before Rodney, who was playing cards, turned to me and said,

"If I were you young brotha, I would knock that out. She's asking for it. Plus, her husband is gone TDY for two months. Nobody will ever know."

TDY is an acronym for temporary duty. Many people on base were assigned to places all over the world for as short as one week and sometimes as long as three months.

I thanked him for his street wisdom and saw myself out of the door. It was late, and all I wanted to do was hit the sack. I did think about what Rodney said. Brandy was fine, but I wasn't going to press my young luck. I figured I was blessed to just be in her company.

The next day after work Brandy showed up at my room. She was smelling good and looking good. I wanted to grab her right there in the door, but I maintained my composure and welcomed her in like a gentleman. She walked into my room and gave me a hug and waited for me to get ready. There were two chairs and my bed to sit on. I offered Brandy a seat on the chair, but she sat on my bed instead. I felt a lump the size of an apple in my throat, and I got a little dizzy. I really didn't know what to say or think, so I walked quickly to the bathroom to finish getting ready. I started talking to myself the way I had done on the bus to San Antonio, pumping myself up psychologically to handle this situation. When I came out of the bathroom, I looked at her, and she looked at me—deeply—with her light brown eyes. I then moved my eyes down from her face to check out her fit. Brandy had on a white casual blouse with tight black jeans, but she made that simple outfit look like it was straight out of *Vogue* magazine, and she knew it.

Before I could open my mouth to say anything, she got off the bed and moved toward me. I felt pursued, even cornered. My hands started sweating; I was speechless. This woman had to be at least twenty-five years old. I was only nineteen. Admittedly, I didn't know how to handle an older woman. Somehow, I was able to squeak out the words "You look real nice tonight. Ready to go?" Rodney would have killed me had he found out what I did. She nodded yes, and we walked out of the door together. That whole night Brandy stayed very close to me. Her vibes were telling me to make a move, but to my surprise, I discovered that I had actually developed an ethic about relationships. I couldn't point to a time or place when this happened, but obviously somewhere deep in my psyche I knew it wasn't right to mess around with a married woman. Though the ethic was easy to understand, my body was communicating a totally different message. Praise God, my body didn't win out. Instead, I realized that I had the power to change the scenario, so wisely, I stayed in my place and kept everything on the up and up. We had a good time that night, and I'll never forget how jovial and intelligent she was. It wasn't her outer beauty that attracted me to her, at least not all the way; really, it was something about her personality and concern for people that got me.

She seemed to be a good woman, so it angered me that her husband was treating her like a dog. I wanted to rescue her from him.

When we returned from the movies, all the fellas were watching me as I got out of her car. Brandy got out, gave me a sensuous hug, and told me that she would see me the next day. I walked back to the dorm, getting big props from the fellas. Rodney followed me up the stairs.

"Did you get that?"

"No. She's married, man!"

"Okay, young blood, but I know she wants you, and you want her!"

Without indulging his curiosity I walked into my room, closing Rodney out of mind at least for the night.

Brandy and I spent a lot of time together after that. She became a real good friend. Within two months, her husband returned from his temporary duty overseas, and our time decreased dramatically, for good reason: her man was back and hopefully, for his sake, the two of them were getting their relationship together. There were a lot of guys just waiting in the bank to see what was going to happen.

In the meantime, I made new friends and counted my time with Brandy as a blessing. She had been there at just the right time for me. When I came to the base, I didn't know a soul; she had ushered me into the limelight there.

I felt good about not making a fool out of myself by doing something I would have regretted later in life. From that time on I never mentioned her name to anyone. I saw her from time to time, and she would always smile and wave at me. I wished several times that her husband would disappear, but he never did. I think Brandy and her husband's relationship improved. As for me, I was glad that I didn't start a web of chaos. I had a clean conscience.

Chapter 21

"Who can find a virtuous woman?" Proverbs 31:10

Looking for Love

After several months and a couple of bad and dangerous relationships with Louisiana ladies, I began to feel at home at Barksdale. The bad relationships were probably due to my immaturity. Rather than looking for a relationship, I should have been developing myself. Instead, I tried to fill that empty space in my life with women. Unfortunately, many of these women were inwardly empty too, though they were stunningly attractive on the outside. So my relationships were mostly lust driven. Lilly was an example. I would even say that I cared about her, but the situation just wasn't right, for it seemed to me that she wanted to live the ghetto life that I was trying to overcome. Brandy had been the only woman that I had met in Louisiana who was everything I would have wanted in a woman, but she was married.

So my last shot at finding a good, educated woman would be at Grambling State University, where a few of the fellas and I would occasionally visit. Grambling had a reputation for having some fine women, but more than that, I knew that the women at Grambling were trying to get something out of life. Surely, there had to be more substance among the Grambling women than what I had found in the others that I dated.

I loved going to Grambling. Visiting the school reminded me of the life I could have had, with one exception. Had I attended college, I would have been a sophomore that year, and very few sophomores had cars at Grambling. I don't know if I could have survived in college without a car especially since I thought that college women only wanted to date guys with cars. I had one, so finding a honey wasn't going to be hard. I simply turned up the music in my EXP and rolled the windows down. My partner sat on the passenger side, and we both leaned way back in our seats, cruising about five miles an hour down the busiest street on campus. The women would wave and flirt, which we would play off by turning our heads in another direction until we saw someone we liked.

The crew from Barksdale also would get together to watch the frats pledge. It was always comical to see what these guys would do to become an Alpha, Kappa, or Omega. All these frats were honorable, but the humiliation involved in getting into them was not worth it to me. We had some crazy, fun-filled nights at Grambling, and I was cool and respected. That felt good.

I was having so much fun that I decided to apply for an early discharge so I could attend Grambling. I yearned to experience college campus life: to go to the football games, to sleep in the dorms, to attend classes like a regular student. But none of that ever happened.

I had a bad mouth and a quick temper, which got worse when I joined the military. For some reason, I felt tougher and almost invincible in the company of other tough guys. Like them, I was always ready for a fight with the locals who didn't like us military guys. That made it was easy to get into a good fight. I also felt I was better than the locals because I was in the military. As much as I wanted to leave some of the ghetto mentality behind, it still crept up on me.

Prior to my Grambling experience, I was with Lilly, a local girl that I really liked. She was with her cousin, Candy, at the movies. I met her there to pick her up. When I arrived, I saw Candy's boyfriend posted up on a police car with his hands behind his back. For some reason, he glanced in my direction and saw me looking at him as I drove by. Just then the worst came out in me. I rolled my tinted, black window down and glared at him with the kind of stare that starts a fight in the streets. Candy's boyfriend was notorious for beating her, and I had heard about it. My stare was acknowledgement from me to him that he was a straight out punk.

I drove away slowly, making sure he saw me; then I parked across from the movie theater. By that time, one of my boys, Horace, had showed up. He was a short, slender brother from New Jersey, who was just as cocky and ignorant as I, and always down with a fight. We talked for a while and just chilled as I waited for Lilly to come out of the movies. As we were about to wrap up our conversation, I noticed two people coming toward me: Lilly, who was walking, and Candy's boyfriend, who was creeping in his red Mitsubishi truck. I eyed Horace, and it was on. We were set to kick some Shreveport behind. As Lilly approached me, I put my arm around her and escorted her to the passenger side of my car. Meanwhile, Horace was watching my back.

As soon as I opened the door for Lilly, these gherri curl Negroes pulled up in the truck, and Candy's boyfriend jumped out and stood about three or four feet from my car. That was too close for me. He had crossed the boundary. So I walked to my side of the car along with Horace and waited for him to say something.

"Well, what's up my man?"

"What? You got a problem with me nigga? Was you looking at me?" he answered.

"Yeah...and?"

Immediately, Horace began to walk to his car to get a bat, but I saw one of the homeboy's reach for something too. So I stopped Horace and challenged "Carefree Curl" to a fight right then.

"Don't get your boys involved! Let's do this. Me and you, right now," I urged.

He looked around at the gathering crowd and saw that the police hadn't even left yet, so it wouldn't be cool to do anything stupid—at least not at that point.

"Naw, man," he replied.

"Yeah. That's what I thought. You might hit your girl, but I ain't your girl."

Why did I say that? I just knew it was on then. He looked surprised that I mentioned his personal business in the street. I was surprised that I did too, but my ego was on the roll, and I had to back it up. All the while, Candy tried to talk some sense into him, which seemed to work for a minute. Then suddenly, he waved to his clique, and they all jumped into his truck and drove off. Surely, I showed him, I thought. I gave Horace some daps, and we parted, expecting to see each other later on base. I got into my car and drove off.

Thinking that the whole scenario was over, I drove along, talking to Lilly and slowing down at the approaching red light. Pulling to a stop, I turned to look at Lilly and was surprised to see "Carefree Curl" roll up with his clique in the red truck on her side of the car. Instantly, he jumped out of the truck, pulled his seat back, and grabbed a shotgun. He's trying to kill me, I said to myself. I pressed the pedal with my full weight and sped through that red light. The tires screeched as I spun the wheel to turn down a dark street. He jumped back into his truck and came speeding through the red light after me.

The chase was on. I tried to out drive him and his boys, but it was difficult. Then he began to shoot at me. All I could do was tell Lilly to duck while I tried to out maneuver his truck. I swerved left and then right for several miles, trying to dodge the loud blasts coming from his shotgun. I thought I heard a bullet had hit my car. Why I was concerned about the car at that point I don't know. Eventually, I out maneuvered him and made it to Lilly's house where we ran inside and called the police. Then I stepped back outside like a crazy man, hoping that he would drive by, but he never did. I was furious because I thought he had hit my brand-new Escort EXP.

The next day, I went to the courthouse to put a restraining order on him. He was arrested within two days; Horace and I appeared in court to press charges. It turned out that Candy's boyfriend had a long record, and the judge was sick of seeing him, so he was automatically fined and sent to jail for a couple of days.

I began to wake up and realize that I was hanging out with the wrong local people. Life hadn't been quite that crazy in Flint, and here I was about to get killed in Louisiana. I knew I had to change my social group quick to one with a little bit more class and wisdom than my counterparts had in Shreveport. At Grambling I hoped to find such a group, but unfortunately, the wild campus parties there weren't very different. When I realized that, I began to lose hope.

Then one weekend my dorm partners asked me to ride to Grambling with them to attend a party. I was completely burned out on parties and didn't want to go, though I still enjoyed the campus atmosphere. They managed to persuade me, and I followed the caravan. When we got there, it was like all the other parties—hot, sweaty, and packed. I wasn't in the building ten minutes before I copped a bad attitude and decided to wait in my car for everyone. I just didn't want to ruin the night for the others by standing around sulking. One of my homeys from the base, Sean, walked back to the car with me.

As we sat in the car talking about life in the fast lane, I noticed a few young ladies approaching us. My windows were tinted extremely dark, so they couldn't see in the car, but I could clearly see them. I could hear them talking too because my window was cracked. Walking right up on my ride without even knowing who I was, one of them surprised me when she bent down toward my cracked window and said,

"Excuse me. I noticed your car plates. Are you from Michigan?"

I hadn't thought about it, but I did have Michigan car plates.

Unfortunately, I really wasn't in the mood to talk to her. I rudely replied, "Yes."

"Oh, I'm from Detroit," she said. "It was just good to see someone else from Michigan. Sorry to bother you."

Then she walked off with her friends. I felt so bad for being rude, and I hadn't really gotten a good look at her, so I decided to swallow my pride and try to redeem myself. It was sprinkling outside, but it looked as if it were going to really rain. So using that as an opener, I yelled to her from across the parking lot, "Excuse me. Looks like it's about to rain. Would you like a ride back to your dorm?" Surprisingly, she said yes and walked back and got into the car. I watched her girlfriends watching me. I think they even wrote down my license plate number. Soon we arrived at her dorm, and she got out.

"What's your name?" I asked.

"Janice."

I returned the favor by giving her my name although she never asked. Then I went for the big time.

"I'd like to call you sometime. Why don't you give me your number?" Janice hesitated for a minute like she was studying me. Then she gave me the digits. I wrote her number down on the back of some old paper in the car and placed it in my wallet.

I drove back to the party and waited with Sean for the rest of the crew. They were all unsuccessful that night. Not one person had gotten a number or a dance. I, on the other hand, had gotten a number simply by chillin' in my car. I bragged all night about that. It was actually funny that so much effort went into the night, and no one was able to get one phone number.

When I got back to Shreveport, I thought about the possibilities and decided to call Janice the next day. She answered, and I was pleasantly surprised to find that this young lady was sharp and aggressive. I hadn't met any young lady my age who was so career-conscious. I really enjoyed talking to her, and she seemed to enjoy talking to me.

Before too long, Janice and I were talking on the phone almost every night. I was nineteen and very aggressive. I had dreams and visions of a future as an entrepreneur. I was very interested in sports clothes and figured that Shreveport/Bossier needed a classy clothing store. So I began to do research about the area and idea. Janice was totally impressed with the whole idea. The more I discussed the store, the more she advised me. She often complimented me on my drive in taking chances and going after whatever I wanted, letting me know how much she admired me. She was right; that was me all over. The tougher the challenge, the more drive I had to make it happen. Risk was not an issue for me. "Nevlynn, you are going to be rich one day. I know it," Janice would say.

With that kind of confidence coming from her, I believed Janice and I were meant to be; we were connected. The many telephone conversations and her willingness to participate in my dream for success caused me to fall for her. We dated for almost a year and a half—time enough, I thought, for me to know that Janice was the one for me. We got along, and we had a lot of fun. She was my visionary partner. I figured that was all a couple needed.

During one of our times together, while Janice and I were in my dorm room watching television and hugging and cuddling each other, I felt a little nudge from her and turned to look directly in her face so she would know she had my complete attention. She began to tell me intimate details about her ordeal with her family, saying that her grandmother and father were manipulative, controlling, and insensitive people and giving me plenty of examples to back her statement. Immediately, I felt anger toward them. How dare they mistreat such a sweet young lady like this? I thought to myself. She went on to say that she felt belittled and left out all the time. According to Janice, no matter how hard she tried, her grandmother and father were never pleased with anything she did or any decision she made.

Her grandmother had adopted Janice and her siblings after their parents abandoned them at a young age. I could tell Janice was still healing from the pain of being abandoned. To some degree, I could relate because my father had bugged out on my mom and me. But mine was nothing like Janice's childhood.

Janice continued, "Nevlynn, would you protect me from my family? They try to control everything I do."

Without thinking rationally, I declared to Janice with confidence that I was the man for the job. All I wanted to do was see her happy. If I could protect Janice from her mean, insensitive, controlling family, surely she would love me always. I had just left a family situation in which my mother seemed to be in the same dilemma. Mom was the family hero, and she worked hard—many times unconsciously—to remain the hero. But just like Janice, Mom could never do enough to please anyone. I had watched my grandparents and my mom's siblings use and abuse her while I helplessly stood by, never quite able to intervene and save her. But now I thought, "I have the power to protect Janice. I will never allow her to get hurt by them again."

Not long after our conversation, I received orders to go to Anchorage, Alaska. I asked Janice to marry me, and she accepted. I couldn't think of anyone else that I would want to spend my entire life with. I was determined to get to Alaska to make everything right for us. We were both young and ready for the world.

We would spend the next nine years of our lives together and then divorce. Unfortunately, the very thing that I felt she wanted me to do for her brought chaos into our relationship. Her parents didn't like me, and Janice began to resent me for trying to protect her. The flaw with the whole situation was that I assumed I could save her, which I couldn't. Over time she became very dissatisfied with our relationship and began to make choices that I disagreed with. But I gave that marriage my best, and I don't regret one day of it because it made me a better man. I only regret the pain I endured during the divorce process.

Chapter 22

"And though she spoke to Joseph day after day, he refused to go to bed with her or even be with her." Genesis 39:10

Harassment

There came a time in my mother's life when she wasn't at her best. She needed some time away from her activities, and decided to come and visit my wife and me in Anchorage. While she was there, I realized that my mother did not have any medical insurance, so I went about the proper procedure to designate her as one of my dependents. Things were looking good until Sergeant Robinson got involved. Then what I thought would be a simple process turned out to be one of most challenging things I had ever faced.

Sgt. Robinson was a tall, medium-weight, white woman, with brown, stringy hair, and she was a true control freak. Although she was married to a white man, she had a thing for black men. This woman would frequently harass me by pinching and patting me on the butt, and asking me questions about black male sexuality. "Are black men really big?" "I bet you are good in bed, aren't you?" The comments and touching really pissed me off, but there was little I could do because everyone in the office was scared of her. So I tried to ignore her. Unfortunately, that didn't help. She took my ignoring her as a challenge, and one day walked up real close to me so I could feel her body while she asked me business questions. I was several ranks below her, so anything I accused her of would be my word against hers in a military judicial system that really sucked, favoring rank unless there was hard evidence to challenge it. Since I could find no one in my office who was willing to testify for me, I was left on my own to deal with her. My strategy was to try to avoid Sgt. Robinson, but that only her all the more. So I knew it was just a matter of time before she would find a way to do something bad to me. When I looked up one day and saw her standing in the door of the Security Police office, I knew by her posture that something was about to happen.

"Airman Johnson, I need to speak to you ASAP."

Leaving mom with the insurance paperwork and assuring her that everything was fine, I followed Sgt. Robinson to her office. She told me to close the door.

"What exactly does your mother need a medical card for?" she demanded to know. "She has a fur coat on. Can't she afford to pay for her own insurance? Why didn't you ask our permission to apply for this card?"

I responded defensively, "I did ask for permission. Sergeant Justus approved the application. Look at it. He signed it."

Luckily I had brought a copy, but surprisingly, rushing to get my mother to the next step, I had forgotten to sign the form myself.

Sgt. Robinson questioned and requisitioned me for almost an hour—so long, in fact, that I began to worry about my mom. This was her first time on the base, and I knew that the military environment could be a little intimidating. When I left Sgt. Robinson's office, I saw my mother sitting in the front office and walked over to her and gave her a hug.

"Is everything all right?" she asked.

I said calmly, "Yes, Mom, just a little misunderstanding."

I grabbed my coat and took her back to the condo. When I returned, Sgt. Robinson had the lynch mob ready. She ordered me back to her office, and with Sgt. Justus and a high-ranking civilian as witnesses, she charged me with defrauding the government and recommended an Article 15—a military write-up that goes into one's record—and a discharge. I stood there in shock, unable to believe what I was hearing. In less than two years in the air force I was faced with one of the worst reprimands given by the United States military. I was totally disappointed in the system and the lack of justice from my supervisors, particularly Sgt. Justus.

Mom refused to take anything from the government after that incident, and that's when I knew I wanted out of the air force, but I couldn't do anything about it. I was a lame duck being prepared for the kill. For days following that event, I walked on eggshells at the office with my every move watched and scrutinized, too scared to do anything. Just getting up in the morning to go to work became a real task. I knew that my charge was based on my refusal to accept Sgt. Robinson's sexual advances and not on credible evidence but, but I couldn't prove it, and no ideas or solutions came to mind. Eventually, Mom went home because she didn't want to be a burden, which caused my resentment to grow even greater towards Sgt. Robinson and the injustice of my situation.

Then it occurred to me that I had a grandfather who was a retired, full bird colonel. He was my dad's real father; I had met him at Dad's funeral a few years back. Though he and my dad never really had a relationship, he had told me after the funeral to call him if I ever needed help.

My grandfather was excited to hear from me. I explained the situation to him, and he promised to take care of it. Less than a week after our conversation I was called into the section commander's office. When I walked in, the commander of our section immediately apologized for the situation, even offering to get my mother an I.D. card. But it was too late by then; Mom had gone home. At the end of our conversation, it was understood that the charges against me would be dropped and that I would be transferred to another section immediately. I had struggled through this intense situation for three months, and in a matter of one week my entire air force career had changed again. Everything happened just as the section commander said, and Sgt. Robinson never said another word to me.

I had experienced racism and sexual harassment in the workplace, which was trying, but I had persevered, for I had no other choice. Two things saved me. First, Terry Justus' signature was on the form, and mine was not, but as my superior, he was responsible for reviewing my work prior to approving it. His signature indicated his approval. In order to successfully charge me with defrauding the government, Sgt. Robinson and the others would have had to charge Sgt. Justus too, but Sgt. Robinson was not willing to do that. That was the racism.

Second, my grandfather's influence saved me. Apparently, my grandfather had a friend in Anchorage who was a general. This general called the base commander to inquire about my case. When a general in any branch of the military gets involved with anything, that is hot stuff. Really, I think that's what did it. Even in the military, it's all about who you know. The base general could not give my grandfather's friend any rational reason for why I was being charged with an Article 15, so the charges were dropped, and several people were verbally reprimanded in the chain of command, including Sgt. Robinson.

After I was transferred, life got much better for me. I enjoyed my new boss—another white woman—as well as my new co-workers. It was ironic to be placed under the supervision of another white woman—Brenda was her name—but she was the reason I was able to let go of the past and move forward. By far, she was the best supervisor and friend I ever had while working on Elmendorf Air Force Base. To this day I attribute much of my healing to her.

PART SIX

Transformation

Chapter 23

"With man this is impossible, but not with God; all things are possible with God." Mark 10:27

Persistence

It was no secret that I wanted to make it big in life. I thought singing and the music industry would be my shot. When I was younger, I had always dreamed of being a singer, but it was just a dream because I had no plans to pursue singing. My only experience had been singing to my family and friends, or in the shower. That was it. Twice during middle school, I had been given singing parts in musicals. So now I was thinking that if I could become wealthy doing something I enjoyed, my life would be fun and financially secure. Nothing would stop me from pursuing that vision; at least that's what I thought.

I became interested in music after hanging out with a guy who really was a gifted musician. After we did a few cuts together I felt that I had the talent to succeed in the music industry, so I temporarily dropped my retail store idea to pursue music in Anchorage, where another friend—Ron—encouraged my singing career. He spent a lot of time teaching me the skills of the music business, and once I learned them, I was on my way. I went as far as producing a single that was played on the radio in Anchorage, which opened the door for me to be the warm-up act for three groups: Troop, Envogue, and Evelyn Champaign King.

While I was busy focusing on music, something else was about to happen for which I was totally unprepared. A white woman named Ruth Orr worked with me. She was a tall, skinny blonde with a very meek disposition, real cool, down to earth and easy to talk to and to be around. Everyone in the office adored her. She was engaged to a real nice fellow too who seemed to be the perfect kind of guy for her with a disposition that matched hers and a real compassion for people. If there were a couple to emulate on base, Ruth and her fiancé were definitely that couple.

Often Ruth would walk over to my desk and talk to me about my music, the subject I enjoyed talking about the most. But I didn't find out what her motive was until lunch one afternoon, when she brought up the subject of church and God. I wasn't shocked because I knew that she was a Christian, and I thought at first that she was going to tell me about hell or make me feel guilty about my pagan goals in life, but she didn't. Ruth's conversation was brief, yet potent. She only talked enough about spirituality to get me interested, and then she switched the subject. Before lunch was over, Ruth had managed to invite me to her church. I admired her for extending the invitation, but I wasn't quite ready to attend anyone's church. I had just gotten through a crisis, and life was looking good, so I rationalized that I didn't need to attend church because God was obviously blessing me already. Ruth was also attending a white Baptist church, which I wasn't too crazy about visiting. I was quite overwhelmed just thinking about it, having heard about Ruth's pastor and how radically conservative he was on political and social issues. I thought it best to politely reject her offer since I knew in my heart that I would never attend her church. It was hard enough for me to visit a black church.

I thought that turning her down would stop the invites, but Ruth persistently found different ways to invite me, and I just as persistently would come up with a lame excuse not to attend. After months and months of trying to reel me in to visit her church, Ruth finally broke me, but in a gentle way—through her consistency and kindness. She invited my wife and me to see a movie at her church with her and her fiancé. I thought to myself, "A movie. What kind of church shows movies?" Curiosity had me. I had to see what this movie was about. Finally, I could appease my workmate.

It was a beautiful and cool Wednesday evening when I visited the Anchorage Baptist Temple. I had almost been tempted to stay home that night to record a new song, but growing more and more curious, I went with Janice and met Ruth and her fiancé in the church sanctuary around 7:30 p.m. Like in many churches, the people there were hospitable. White male ushers greeted us at the door, a little surprised that we were visiting. I knew that our color had a lot to do with it since there were very few blacks that attended this church. As a matter of fact, I can't remember any blacks in the church that night.

Anchorage Baptist Temple was the largest church in the state, and it was led by a southerner from Tennessee named Tom Williams, a very provocative preacher in the community. Anchorage Temple drew many of its members from the local military installations, and was the most influential political body in the city, which was mostly composed of white, right-wing Christian evangelicals. Though the church was big, there was a small church friendliness about it, and I noticed with interest that many of the members had a southern drawl.

My wife and I found seats directly behind Ruth, who was elated that I had actually kept my word about showing up. We talked briefly before the movie started. Once it did, I was immediately drawn to the action. The movie was based on the stories in the Bible about the last days. I had been duped, I thought to myself. I wasn't expecting to see an end of the world presentation. I wanted to leave, but I was too nervous to get up. Besides, I had really gotten interested in the plot and before I knew it, I was sucked into the action. By the time the movie ended, I was sure that I had missed out on something in life—something spiritual.

As the lights slowly brightened, Reverend Williams, a tall, slender white man, wearing a tailor-made gray wool suit, walked up to the microphone and began to speak. He pointed his finger at the audience with conviction and challenged us all to think about our salvation. It felt like he was talking directly to me. He asked two questions.

"If you died tonight would you go to heaven or hell?"

The second question was a follow up to the first.

"Do you know Jesus Christ as your savior?"

Seriously, up to that point in my life, I had never thought about either heaven or hell. My life had been centered on Janice and music. As far as I was concerned the United States Air Force and my past experiences in Flint were my hell.

Suddenly, as the music began to play, ReverendWilliams asked people to give their lives to Jesus Christ by walking down the aisle. The audience stood up, and as I looked over to my wife, I saw tears in her eyes. The next thing I knew she was walking toward the preacher. I stood there for a moment thinking it through. "Do I want to do this?" What does it mean to give myself to Jesus Christ?" What will I have to give up?" I was left all alone to think about my spiritual future. As the music subsided, I decided to do what my wife did. I side-stepped into the aisle, walking to the front of the church where I knelt down near my wife and waited for further instructions. Soon a man in a dark gray suit knelt beside me and said, "Are you here to give your life to Jesus Christ?" I nodded in approval; then the man said, "Pray this prayer with me: 'Dear Lord, I am a sinner, and I ask Jesus into my life right now. I believe that Jesus is your Son, and that He was crucified and raised from the dead for my salvation. Come into my heart now Jesus, and save me.'" After I repeated the prayer, I was asked to fill out some paperwork; then Janice and I were allowed to leave. Something happened to me that day that can't quite be put into words. I knew my life had just changed forever, but I didn't know how.

Ruth had managed to get my wife and me to church to watch a movie, and through that we both ended up accepting Jesus Christ as our savior. Instinctively, I knew I had habits that would have to change. I wasn't sure what would happen or when the change would come. I just knew that somehow my private and public life would be impacted by this decision.

The next day at work I saw Ruth, who was just beaming with excitement and telling everyone in the office that my wife and I had been saved. Immediately, people began to expect different things from me, and I suddenly felt as if I had to be perfect around the office. Slowly, I began to watch my words around people because I was concerned that I would give God a bad name. Everyone around me knew that I cursed. That stopped! My temper was a little short, and that changed too. Some of the change was easy because I did want to change. My decision to become a Christian was giving me an excuse to start over and live life the way it was supposed to be lived. Life had to get better now that I belonged to Jesus Christ.

Chapter 24

"Therefore, if anyone is in Christ, he is a new creation."

A New Faith

To be quite frank, the challenge of changing my lifestyle to fit the Christian framework was hard. Prior to my church experience in Anchorage, I had had no real substantial spiritual development. My mother had become a Christian, but she was still in the process of learning, herself. Therefore, I had no true church or Christian tradition in my background. As a result, everything that I learned in Alaska was relatively new. It was the same for my wife. We were both in the dark as it related to our faith and the new expectations.

As far as a church community was concerned, we didn't feel quite comfortable at the Anchorage Baptist Temple. For one thing, the culture was radically different than what I was used to. An aura of privilege prevailed in the church, and the people didn't seem to be in touch with the suffering, the lost, or the oppressed. Though my church background was rather empty, I did recognize quickly that something was not right in this church with the communication of God's word, for it seemed geared mostly to middle class values. So this restlessness led both Janice and me to visit other churches in town.

During this process, many changes began to happen in our home as both my wife and I realized that our lives had to be cleaned up. One of the first things that I decided would have to go was our secular music.

Bobby Brown, Whitney Houston, Al B. Sure (which was my favorite CD), New Edition, Heavy D, and even MC Hammer all had to go into a big, black trash bag. Secular music was not beneficial to our souls and minds, I had concluded. I am not sure that my wife fully agreed, but I think she saw that my heart was in the right place. "Do we have to throw all of them away?" she asked. "I think we do," I replied. My entire collection of rhythm and blues went to the garbage dump in a matter of seconds.

"To follow Christ, we must be perfect and pure; today's music is evil and damaging to the mind," is what I had heard a preacher say. I figured he was right. After all, the man was a preacher. So all my "evil" music, though I loved it, was thrown away.

I also had a mouth like a sailor. After hanging around a few Christian people and listening to their conversation, I knew that I had to change mine. I didn't hear "good Christians" use profanity, but I had grown up with profanity in my family—as the primary language in many instances—so using profanity was not a moral or immoral issue with me. Rather, it was a way to strongly communicate a message. "Let your yes be yes, and your no be no," I often heard from preachers in the pulpit, so I knew I had to clean up my mouth. My wife followed suit, without much nudging from me.

The morals and values of the church confronted our private and public conduct. Our first lesson was not learning to love Jesus but changing from our wicked ways. There were many other things I wanted to change, but it just seemed too difficult to do. Yet within a year we had improved a lot in our conduct and character. But, in many respects it was hard to change patterns that we were so used to.

In the process of changing conduct, finding the appropriate church was an additional job. This by far was the most difficult task. There were all types of churches: Independent Baptist, Southern Baptist, Presbyterian, Episcopalian, African Methodist Episcopal, Christian Methodist Episcopal, Pentecostal, Church of God in Christ, and many more. Which was the right one? Which church was the best? My young wife and I questioned this often. We both had charismatic backgrounds, though mine was more limited than hers. And I definitely preferred less demonstrative churches because of a bad childhood experience. There was no way I was going to have anyone force me to speak in tongues.

Ironically, while sitting home after dinner one night, Janice and I saw a television program broadcast by a local, black, charismatic preacher who seemed to know his Bible. What was most interesting about his teaching was his preoccupation with healing and prosperity. Considering that I was in the air force with low pay, I wanted to know more about this God who could create finance through faith. My wife was curious about the money-making opportunity herself, so one morning we decided to visit this church.

The church building was a metal, A-frame structure, located in an open warehouse-type facility. When I walked in the first thing I saw were books and tapes with such titles as *Conquering Poverty, God is in the Business of Blessing, Ask and Believe*, and *Faith and Healing*. All the books attracted me, and I wanted to read every one of them, but the costs prohibited that.

After realizing we were visitors, someone tapped Janice and me on the shoulder and politely ushered us into the sanctuary where there were probably a hundred or so people of all nationalities standing and praising the Lord and reading song lyrics from a screen overhead. They didn't seem ashamed of crying, waving their hands, or even jumping up and down, which reminded me of my Pentecostal past, but the music and atmosphere here were different.

When everyone settled down, Janice and I found seats near the front of the church where we could clearly hear what the preacher was saying. Then a woman, who turned out to be the preacher's wife, moved swiftly to the front of the church. Once she positioned herself, the preacher began to speak in tongues—an unknown spiritual language—and she translated his spiritual message. My mother had spoken in an unknown tongue before, so this was not new to me. What was new, however, was the interpretation. I was naïve, but not so much that I didn't think of how convenient it was for the preacher's wife to be the interpreter of his spiritual message, especially since no one else knew what the heck this brother was saying. It seemed a little funny to me, but I went along with it.

After the translation, the preacher began talking about faith and prosperity. (By the way, his wife's translation backed up the message.) The preacher discussed the blessed life of the believer.

"If you are a believer, you shouldn't be sick. We are healed by his stripes. What are you still doing sick?" he asked.

It made perfectly good sense to me, though had I been struck with an illness, I might have challenged his theology.

"If you want a Mercedes, don't you think God wants his children to have the best? You are the children of a king. A king doesn't give his children junk. Ask for the Mercedes in faith, and see what God does."

As young and foolish as I was, I believed. I asked and asked for the Mercedes, but I haven't gotten it yet. It could have been my lack of faith, but I doubt it. It wasn't long after this that the preacher asked the unsaved to come to the front of the church. Although Janice and I had already been saved at the Anchorage Baptist Temple, we went through the process again. The church welcomed us and invited us to be a part of their church family. Two people greeted us as we were taken to the back for new members' processing, and shortly thereafter Janice and I were separated, and I was moved to a private room where yet another stranger was waiting to process me.

"Do you speak in tongues?" he asked.

"No," I quickly replied. Right then I started thinking about my experience in the tent revival and other experiences in Pentecostal churches.

"Speaking in tongues is a gift. If you want it, claim it, and just start speaking. It will probably sound childlike in the beginning, but that's how most people start out," he instructed me.

By now I am thinking either I am crazy or this guy is crazy. I'm not speaking in tongues, I tell myself. Then, without warning, this guy went into a trance and starting speaking in tongues. It sounded like childish babble, just as he said, but I remained unconvinced. Again, he entered a hypnotic state and started speaking, then came out of his trance just as quickly as he had entered it.

"Try it. You can do it," he encouraged me.

After watching for a while, I said, "What the heck?" Soon, I was babbling. I had no idea what I was saying, nor did he. As far as I know, God could have been communicating some great truth, but we will never know.

I was congratulated and hugged, then sent to the concourse to wait for my wife. While I waited I thumbed through the books that had caught my attention earlier. Within minutes, Janice strolled out of the room, and we both looked at each other conveying a silent signal that we both wanted to leave. We visited that church for a while, but once again we knew that we had not found our church home.

My newfound faith gave my mother so much pleasure. She was elated that her son had finally seen the light, and it occurred to me that Mom's desire all the while had been for my wife and me to be Christians. We were the only couple in the family that had the appearance of marital health, and Mom really wanted our marriage to work. Christianity would help it, I'm sure she believed. She also tried to aid it along by calling my wife often in hopes that their friendship would get stronger, which my wife didn't seem to mind that at all. After all, she wanted to have a mother, so she adopted mine. It was special to see the relationship between those two grow. I got the sense that my marriage would be stronger if Mom and my wife were close. Things seemed to be going well, and now all we needed was a church.

The next church that we visited was a prophetic church that a friend talked me into visiting. By that time, it was known around base that I had become a Christian, and Keith saw the growth in me and felt an obligation to help me see more of the light. I agreed to visit his church, which to my surprise was very racially mixed. This time the pastor was white, and his wife was quite involved in the church leadership. They were both called prophets. I had read about prophets in the Bible and found that they were used by God to warn the Israelites that their future would be gloomy if they continued to rebel. Beyond that I guess

I thought of prophets as fortunetellers. It seemed as though these preachers were fortunetellers more than prophets. The whole thing was a little confusing to Janice and me.

When Janice and I arrived at the church, we sat in the middle, trying to hide in the crowd. That was difficult, though, because there were only forty or fifty people there. The church was located in a storefront, commercial building and held its service in an open room with folding chairs set up audience-style. Janice and I were obvious and uncomfortable. Just as service was about to begin the pastor received a revelation and pointed to us. I believe it was something about prosperity too. It was nice to know that God was going to bless us with prosperity, but after visiting that church for a while Janice and I decided to move on. The people at the church were awfully friendly, but it just wasn't our speed.

My relationship with Keith fizzled out after we stopped attending his church because he felt that my wife and I were too immature to understand the prophetic teachings; therefore, we were too immature to be his friends. I was really looking for a friend, too, and I thought he would be the one, but our relationship was limited to discussion about prophecy and the Bible. He never had time for anything else.

Finding a good church was becoming very difficult. Then one day I ran into a young lady, who attended a small black Baptist church, that I had met when I was recording music. She had invited my wife and me to her church where her father was the pastor. At first, I wasn't very interested, but after visiting three or four churches, I thought "Why not? We've visited prophetic churches, charismatic, prosperity, and conservative, right churches. What could we lose?" So I decided to visit her church during a Wednesday Bible study when her father, a black southern pastor, was teaching. He reminded me of my grandfather—tall and dark-skinned with a commanding and passionate Southern black drawl. I could tell he loved doing what he was doing. His daughter happened to be there that night and introduced me him. Immediately, I fell in love with him and the friendly people, but I didn't join right away. Instead, I waited for my wife, who felt the same way I did after she visited. Within two weeks, we knew that we had found our church home, and we joined.

The church was a small, brick A-frame with red carpet inside and the smell of mildew in the basement. It was an old, worn church, but the people seemed focused and set on pleasing the Lord. My wife and I had joined a traditional, Southern Baptist, black church. Funny, there were not many black Southern Baptist churches in the state, but we found one in Anchorage, Alaska. I enjoyed the choir and the preaching like never before, and this church became our home away from home. The people loved us, and we loved them.

At Friendship Baptist church my life would make another turn that would affect my marriage and my perspective on the world. It wasn't a planned turn, but one that would surely be the map for my future. Friendship Baptist Church and Reverend James Davis would make a lasting impression on me.

Chapter 25

"And we know that in all things God works for the good of those who love him, who have been called according to his purpose." Romans 8:28

Called

To be called, or not to be called. That's the question. The "call" in the African American religious experience is a significant one. Those who go to church, and many times those who don't, have a sense that they are ultimately subject to God's plan for their lives, no matter how wonderful or pitiful their plight. Simply put, the call is the exchanging of the worldly lifestyle for the holy lifestyle of God. The higher "calling" usually leads to one's assuming the position of pastor-preacher. This was and continues to be in many respects the highest of the highest callings. When a man or woman accepts the calling in the Black church, it is a big deal.

I remember dating a young lady in high school named Toni. Toni was very attractive and two years my senior, and her father was a pastor. Once while talking on the phone, Toni and I began discussing our future careers.

"What do you feel you will be doing when you get older?" she asked.

"I want to be an engineer, or possibly a preacher" I said.

I thought it was a good move considering her father was a pastor, but I was wrong.

"Then you won't be my husband, 'cause I ain't marrying a pastor. My daddy's a pastor, and I couldn't handle it."

That comment bothered me, but I would later understand. Obviously, there were pressure and commitments behind the scenes in a pastor's life that I was unaware of. It looked good from the audience, but there was so much more responsibility involved in the position of pastor than preaching. As a result, the family was impacted by this "calling" too. Toni indicated this in our conversation. It didn't hit me then, but I sure understand now.

After settling into Friendship Baptist, I became a very good friend with another young man by the name of Larry, and he and I took to each other quickly. He was easy to talk to and turned out to be good company, and Janice and I invited him to the house often. One of the things we discussed with each other was our spiritual struggles because we were both considering announcing our call to the ministry.

Week after week, Larry and I were both very involved at church. We often sought counsel from people about our call, and when no one else understood, we were there for each other. Larry was able to discuss a lot with his father, too, which really helped him tremendously. I, on the other hand, had no father to talk to, so Reverend Davis became a surrogate father to me. That was dangerous, and in many ways most ignorant on my part, for I had the silly notion that my pastor would love me and give me Godly advice just as a good father would do. For a variety of reasons, this dream never came to pass, probably because Reverend Davis was too preoccupied with his own goals and objectives as a pastor and a visionary. So my little calling was of no major importance to him. I expected too much out of the relationship, and as a result of my projections, I was let down many times. Still, none of the disappointments mattered. I got from my pastor what I could get and continued to see him as my model of a pastor.

Eventually, Larry felt led to finally accept his calling and notified the pastor. During service the next Sunday, Reverend Davis gave him an opportunity to announce his calling before the congregation. As Larry got up nervously from the pew and walked to the pulpit,

Reverend Davis moved to the side to allow him to speak. In tears, Larry declared with certainty, "I've been struggling with this for so long. I am not going to run anymore. I am accepting my calling to the ministry." The church was on fire. Many people had known Larry from childhood, and openly welcomed the new transition in his life. As I witnessed the support he received from his family and the pastor, I yearned for the same kind of backing. Larry and I, both twenty-one, were two African American young men, catapulted into a world about which we were very naïve. Watching Larry, I knew that my time would come, but I didn't know when.

The desire to announce the calling became a fire burning on the inside, getting more and more difficult to keep to myself. Time and time again, I talked to my wife about it, but she had little to say. I'd ask her about her thoughts, and usually she would merely say, "If God called you, then I will support you." At the time, her comment was comforting, but not totally. Both my wife and I were very ignorant of the responsibilities of such a role.

Less than a year prior to the calling, I had been involved in music and singing at clubs with different groups. Really, Janice and I had only just become new Christians and had not had time to develop our theology before I was thinking about jumping into a pulpit and preaching. I really meant no harm. The desire to make a change in peoples' lives, mixed with the desire to model my pastor, became a drive for me. At the top of the list, I must admit that I really wanted to please God. I wanted God to be pleased with me as a Christian, and what better way to do it than by committing to full-time Christian service. The whole situation was a mystery to Janice and to me, but I was willing to take a chance for the Lord. Since my wife seemed to have no objections to this new commitment, I finally admitted to the pastor that my time had come.

Reverend Davis was happy as a meadowlark. Several weeks prior, Larry had announced his call, and now I was about to do the same. The church was growing, and there was a great need for leaders to teach and disciple. I believe that concern was at the top of his list, but I had no background to be a leader. I was too young and too ignorant to teach anyone anything about the Bible. I had no formal education, no spiritual background, or history. I was merely a young man seeking to please the Lord. *Yet at times, I wondered if I was also trying to please people.* I also believe Reverend Davis was excited about my new calling because I was involved with music, having been tipped off by his daughter about my recording pursuits. Davis loved his choir, and felt that the choir—which his daughter directed—needed to record. Who better to usher the age of Gospel recording into Friendship Baptist than I? For almost a year I wasn't even cognizant of his motives, and what a blow it was to my ego when I found out because I had thought the pastor was genuinely interested in me for me.

Pastor Davis scheduled me to announce the call during a Sunday service after the choir had finished their selections. He announced to the church that God was doing a great work in calling young men to the ministry at Friendship Baptist. Then he looked at me, giving me my cue to get up and make the announcement. I looked at Larry, and he gave me a nod of encouragement. I got up slowly, walked to the pulpit, and quickly announced to the congregation that God had called me to the ministry. Again, the congregation was excited, but I didn't get the support from them that Larry had gotten, which made me a little jealous, but not enough to get me down. Minutes later, Davis announced to the church that I would be doing three trial sermons before I was licensed. I sat down and felt a sense of relief.

After the service, the Pastor Davis took me to his office where we prayed. Then he began to talk to me about my new responsibilities as a minister. Reverend Davis, a retired military man accustomed to shortening names, called me John, short for Johnson, which my wife hated.

"John, you are a nice young man, but we are going to have to change your look. You are a preacher now; you have to look like a preacher. You need to start wearing suits and ties, and we need to get you to teach a class."

Mind you, I hadn't even preached my first sermon, but I was ushered into the world of ministry anyway. I loved sweaters, and really all that I owned were fashionable sweaters. I was immediately stressed about my appearance and lack of teaching knowledge. My wife and I talked about the new changes I would have to make. Neither of us quite understood, but we went along with the plan. Actually, I believe this is when my wife's attitude about the calling began to change.

Soon after my horrible presentations of the gospel, I was licensed. One year after my conversion to my new faith, I was a licensed Baptist minister—May of 1991. The women in the church began to talk to my wife about the responsibilities of a minister's wife, which she hated. I could barely get away with telling her something, much less the church women who had no idea how much she despised someone telling her how to behave or conduct herself. That became a tremendous burden for Janice. Where I welcomed the suggestions, and many times the criticisms, my wife rejected them and rejected the notion of being a minister's wife. What made it worse was when the women of a certain auxiliary asked her to become a Sunday school teacher. It was expected that all ministers' wives would accept a position in the church as a Sunday School teacher. Surprisingly, my wife accepted a teaching position with the eight-year-olds. For a while, I really think she liked it, but it got old quick. I accepted roles as the men's adult Sunday School teacher and the youth teacher for high school teenagers. I loved it. I was able to really get into the Bible at a different level than before. I was borrowing books from Davis frequently. My wife and I matured spiritually and psychologically during this time.

But Janice didn't really appreciate the expectations of a minister or a minister's wife and began to voice her displeasure more and more. She tolerated it because we belonged to a small church, and there were Christian women with whom she spent time who were encouraging to her. They were older women, some the age of her mother. I believe my wife was looking for a mother figure as a result of the lack of maternal nurturing in her life just as much as I was looking for a father figure. The few women that my wife allowed in her circle influenced her greatly, and encouraged me, and there was a minimum of dissension, at least for a while.

Still, every so often, I would hear things like, "Nevlynn, you were called, not me," or "I didn't marry a minister." At times, I was able to handle the comments; at other times, they would stress me. I wasn't quite sure what had happened. I knew that what the people in the church were doing was not all correct, but I believed that I had made the right decision about the calling. We were at a crossroads, but it would take years before my wife and I realized it.

I was given more responsibilities as time went on. Rev Davis began a radio ministry that another minister and I led. I sang in the choir for a while, until the teaching demands became too heavy. Janice and I also attended every church service. Our Sunday would start at 8:15 in the morning, picking up donuts at the grocery store. We'd move on to Sunday School at 9:30, followed by the regular morning service. Church would end at about 2:00 in the afternoon. We'd go to dinner, usually to the same cafeteria every Sunday, with every other black church member in the city. Then we were back for the night service at 5:30. I was still in the air force and attending college full time. Both Janice and I were busy and seemingly doing the right things, working hard to be successful at church and in our professional lives. Unfortunately, we didn't stop to "smell the roses" along the way.

Soon it became apparent that our lack of quality time with one another was causing greater marital conflict. Our normal disagreements turned into heated verbal wars. To take it further, she had an uncanny ability to push me to the edge. Sometimes we would be talking at home about a subject, and if she disagreed, she would make her opinions known by using physical force, brushing up against me, trying to force me to retaliate. It was like she wanted me to hit her. Sometimes I wanted to, but I didn't. Every time we would have an argument like that, I would think about my uncle Jake and my grandfather. I made a vow to myself to never hit my wife, no matter the circumstance. It was hard, but I kept that vow.

One day, we got into a bad argument and Janice bumped me with her body, like she was egging me on to fight. I backed up to regain my balance, but she came at me again. By this time, I knew that it was on. Once and for all, I was going to straighten this mess out. Just as I was about to speak my mind, she reached up and slapped me with force, like she was hitting a stranger. I stood there for minutes looking at her, trying to regain my composure. I was surprised, even shocked. My wife hit me. No, more than that, she slapped me. This woman stood 5' 1", and I was 6' 2". There was also a great disparity in our weight, yet she stood there ready to rumble. I really didn't know what to do. As she took her stance ready to fight, I turned and walked to our bedroom to lie on the bed. That was the only sane thing I could think of doing. I left her there in her fighting stance.

I remember watching her out of the corner of my eyes as I walked to the room, seeing so much anger and bitterness in her eyes. Really, it scared me. As I lay in the bed, I remember thinking, "How did this happen? I promised myself to never get in a violent relationship, but here I am." I studied the situation as long as I could. Then that ghetto Flint voice began to talk to me.

"Listen here, you don't let no woman put her hands on you. Kick her behind. That will teach her." Again the voice said,

"Get up out of this bed and grab her by the neck and put a street whooping on her." Before I knew it, I was up out of the bed, walking down the steps angry and vengeful. As I got to the bottom of the steps, I noticed my wife get up. She seemed to expect something to happen, and for all practical purposes it was about to. But when I looked in her eyes all I could do was say, "Don't ever put your hands on me again, you hear. I mean it, don't ever do it again!" I guess the seriousness of the situation hit her. My wife never said a word; I don't even remember her apologizing, but it never happened again. We had several arguments, many of which I believe went too far verbally, but there was never a physical altercation again.

Many times I believe my wife wanted me to do something crazy so she would have an excuse to divorce me. As crazy as my family background was, I was also determined to make my marriage work. I wasn't going to let anything get in the way of my love for and commitment to her. There were times during our first couple years of marriage that I thought that I had made a mistake. But, as time passed, I believe that we began to appreciate and trust one another. For the first time in our marriage, I believe my wife developed a sense that she couldn't provoke me to leave her, which was good, because I had no intention of going anywhere. After getting through that rough period, in addition to our struggle with the call, I felt that we would make it.

Life was moving on, and quickly I may add, and I found myself faced with another major decision less than one year after my licensing. Should I pursue theological training? After discussing the matter with my pastor, I was convinced that he was not giving me sound advice. He often recommended mail course theological training to me. Reverend Davis would say, "John, you can save a lot of time getting a degree in theology if you read these books and send back a report. In no time you will have your degree, with a little hard work. The best part is that you never have to leave Anchorage." It all sounded good, but for some reason, it didn't fully appeal to me. It seemed every minister at Friendship Baptist, except Larry, had very little advice to give me in regard to theological training. It was an awfully frustrating place to be. I wanted to study to show myself approved, and I knew that I wouldn't be able to do that in Anchorage.

I was one semester away from graduating with a bachelor's degree in personnel administration, and Janice was just as close to completing an associate's degree. She was on a full scholarship at the University of Alaska. The way things were looking there was a good chance the school would offer her a scholarship for her entire bachelor's program, but that would take an additional two years. In less than sixty days, I was going to have to make a decision about separating from the air force. The tension in this decision was whether to leave Alaska or to stay there. With a scholarship in hand for my wife it seemed that staying in Anchorage was the thing to do, but I would not be able to attend seminary.

In the meantime, I sent applications to two seminaries, one in Louisville, Kentucky, and the other in Atlanta, Georgia. To my surprise, the first one to accept me was the Southern Baptist Theological Seminary in Louisville. Southern was one of the most prestigious seminaries in the theological world, and I had heard many things about the school from the administrators at the college I was attending. I got very excited about the possibilities and discussed the issue with my wife. Her position was cold and unwavering. She was not ready to leave Alaska, and she was not giving up a scholarship to move to Kentucky. In many ways I agreed. Either I was going to get out of the air force and stay in Alaska, or I was going to reenlist and face the chance of being shipped somewhere else in the world. One way or another there was no guarantee that we would stay in Anchorage. I prayed about the entire situation, expressed my feelings to my wife and left it there. By that time I was convinced that going to seminary was a necessity if I were going to stay in the ministry.

Almost two weeks later, my wife walked into the house with a blank look on her face. I didn't really know how to take her expression. Then she walked over to me and said, "Nevlynn, let's move to Kentucky. I've been reading about Louisville, and it doesn't seem to be too bad of a place." I was elated, and she knew it. It wouldn't have mattered if we moved to Atlanta or Detroit, just as long as I was able to attend seminary. Of course, there was a compromise. My wife would choose where we would live in Louisville. She was just as determined to have control of finding our home as I was to attend seminary.

In March of 1992 I signed the paperwork to separate from the United States Air Force. Separating was almost as frightening as joining the military had been.

"What will you do out there?" asked my co-workers.

"I will find a job and work like everyone else in the United States," I replied.

It was only then that I realized that so many of my peers had grown very content with the military life. Others were fearful of leaving its protective world. I was different only because I dared to be different. Once again, I was off to a new challenge, but this time it was spiritual. I was leaving the military to learn about God and the Christian ministry.

In May of 1992, my wife and I both graduated from our higher institutions of learning with a great sense of accomplishment. I was proud that I was prepared to take care of my wife and myself. The people at Friendship Baptist offered no real support. As a matter of fact, the famous speech I got from the other ministers including my pastor was, "Watch out for those devils in those seminaries. They'll mess you up." They made it seem like I had just sentenced myself to death, but I knew I had made the right decision.

Janice tried hard to be happy about the move, but she really wasn't. Yet, she was exceedingly joyful to leave Friendship Baptist and all of the expectations of those auxiliary women. Beyond that, she seemed to hold a grudge against me for her having to leave behind the college scholarship. She had interrupted her college education to marry me, and now she was transitioning again because of my desire to attend seminary. I could empathize with her, but I didn't know what else to do. Had she never given the okay, I would have never felt comfortable about making the decision. Her grudge would later turn into bitter resentment.

On June 2, 1992, Janice and I set out on the open road in our gray 1992 Pontiac Grand Prix. As I drove out of the gates of Elmendorf Air Force Base, I waved goodbye to my past and headed toward our future. Though I toyed with the idea of returning to the military as a chaplain, I knew deep in my heart that I would never be a military man again. As we drove over the Alaskan roads, I thought about all that had happened since our move to Alaska. In three short years, I had managed to experience so much. I never intended for life to move the way it did; I was merely trying to make the best of each moment. Now, something new was ahead—a bright future filled with new challenges. Again, I had no idea where it would lead, but I was willing to take the chance. The sad thing was that I hadn't taken the time to really think through all of the past transitions to prepare myself for the new.

Chapter 26

"My eyes fail from weeping, I am in torment within, my heart is poured out on the ground because my people are destroyed."

Lamentations 2:11

Bluegrass Country

The first thing we did when we arrived at River City was visit the seminary. The campus was beautiful, with flowers and trees everywhere, and the crisp, clean feel of an Ivy League school. After walking around for a while and soaking up the vibes on campus, Janice and I were off to see our new apartment on campus. We had made a deal that if it wasn't to her liking we would find a place off-campus to live. As soon as we walked into the apartment, I looked at her and knew that we would be doing some apartment shopping.

It only took us a few days to find one, and we were ecstatic when we did. Our new place was part of a spacious complex, located in the peaceful suburbs. We slept on the carpet our first night there because we had no furniture, but we celebrated anyway by eating a meal we picked up at a fast food place. My first duty as a new resident would be to call the moving company for our things.

I was happy because my wife was pleased. Now that our home was established, the only thing left to do was to find jobs. I knew that I would have a heck of a challenge because I had to schedule my hours around my seminary classes, but somehow, I knew in my soul that things would work out. My wife and I had stepped out on faith, and there was no turning back now.

After looking for two long weeks, I landed a full-time position as an assistant manager with Walden's pharmacy. I was interviewed and hired by the district manager, and started my new position—with no experience in retail—on July 1, 1992. things were working out. My wife even found a job soon after I started working with Walden's. Initially, I had been nervous about finding employment because Janice and I had only saved enough money to pay our bills for two months. I kept hearing an internal voice that repeatedly said, "You are responsible for your family. You've got to find a job." So I was prepared to work anywhere just to say I had a job, but luckily Walden's gave me a chance not only to have a job but to make a living, and the district manager allowed me to schedule my hours around the seminary schedule. The job's flexibility was the good thing, and the pay wasn't bad either. As a matter of fact, I was making more at Walden's than I had ever made in the military. But, with any good thing there are some negative things to deal with, and I was confronted with mine almost immediately.

I had recently left the air force, where I dealt with a racist and sexist supervisor, and for some reason, I thought that life would be better in the corporate world. To my surprise, it wasn't. I was instantly inducted into the world of racism when I was placed in another store after my one-month training period was completed. Once again, I was in an environment where I had to prove my competence as a black man. It didn't matter that I had served in the United States Air Force. It didn't matter to the store management that I was a college graduate. Instead, my color was the primary concern for my co-workers at Walden's.

Mr. White, the store manager, was a well-dressed, overweight, Yuppie type, though his weight didn't seem to be a problem for him. As a matter of fact, I think he felt it was a quality of some sort, for Mr. White, who always bragged on himself, had an ego like no one I ever knew. He also had a beautiful wife and two darling children. I often wondered how he was able to attract such a striking and intelligent woman, but I quickly settled in my mind that it was none of my business. The two of them seemed to be very happy together. My opinions didn't matter.

Mr. White was a very assertive and bossy man, yet at times he was extremely compassionate and understanding. I never was able to figure him out, nor his unique working relationship with the other employees, who seemed to worship him. But I believe that it was the employees' dedication to Mr. White that made his store the most profitable one in the city. Of course, my take on his personality and work style was not the same as the other employees. I just wanted to work myself through seminary and get the heck out of there as soon as I could. But I did realize that the Walden's company was in desperate need of black management. So, not long after I was hired the district manager chose me as a top candidate for a future position in management. This is why I had ended up at Mr. White's store. The district wanted me to be trained by the best. It was ironic: my motive was to get a job to support my family through seminary; the district's motive was to train me to be a future manager. I guess we met each other's need for a while, and for a short time, I did think about pursuing a career with Walden's.

Mr. White's goal was to train me up in the way I should go in Walden's, and he did a great job of it. But there was a real stumbling block for him as well as for the other employees—my race. At one point, the bookkeeper told Mr. White that as far as she was concerned, I was just a black man with a beard, wearing a blue smock. It didn't matter to her or the rest of the employees that I was an assistant manager. Rather, I had to prove my trustworthiness as a black man first, then as a manager, which was a real challenge, and even comical at times. Had it not been for my sense of humor, I wouldn't have made it through many days. I was a young, twenty-three year-old, ready to take on the world. Walden's would definitely be a preparation ground for me.

The real comedy began one day when Mr. White requested an informal meeting with me in the warehouse, which would become our main meeting ground. When I was first notified of the meeting in the warehouse, I thought that Mr. White was going to fire me. I had no idea why, but I had gotten the idea that when a manager invited a brother to the back for a meeting, the meeting usually ended in a dismissal. So I bucked at the meeting, asking why it couldn't take place in the front office. If Mr. White was going to fire me, I wanted the whole store to see. Fortunately, that was not the case. Mr. White simply felt that the warehouse was the most private area in the store.

Anyway, he took me to the warehouse after I had been working there for a short while. After making sure there were no other employees around, Mr. White leaned forward and began talking to me.

"Mr. Johnson, Beth, the bookkeeper gave you a compliment today. You know what she said?"

"No I don't,"

"She said that you were a sharp black man. She told me this morning that you were no longer considered a black man with a beard, wearing a blue smock, but that you were a sharp, black man."

I didn't know whether to take that as a compliment or a slap in the face. I thought to myself, "Why couldn't I simply be considered a sharp person? What did my color have to do with anything?" Realizing what was going on, I put things together quickly. For several months, the store employees and Mr. White had been watching me more than they had been watching everyone else. For several months, my work performance had been evaluated, but more than that, my race and gender were being evaluated. It seems that a group of blue-collar workers was betting on my failure because of my color. To this day, this perception by the white world has affected the very way that I work. I know that when I take a job that I am dispelling myths and stereotypes of black males and that I have to confront all of that mess before I am even considered competent.

Mr. White continued, "Mr. Johnson, a compliment like that coming from Beth is pretty hard to get. Another thing that has impressed us is the fact that you have balanced all the drawers in the store every night, and you have been closing the store on time. Mr. Johnson, this is great. For some reason I didn't think you would cut it. You know, with the condition of your people and all, it's hard to find good black men like you. I just want you to know that you're doing a good job, and you will make a great manager of a store one day if you keep up the good work."

After Mr. White's unique soliloquy, I was left in the stock room speechless. When I regained my composure, I was ready to curse him out for making me out to be some sort of icon for Black America. I was the good nigger, and I guess the other black men were the bad ones. At that moment, I was furious because I didn't want to be the good one, at least not in his eyes. Who made him an authority on good blacks and bad blacks anyhow? His whole arrogance and the rest of the staff's pissed me completely off. Once again, I was experiencing the race issue. Not that I didn't expect it. I merely wanted to be judged based on my job performance, not my race.

That day was a rough one for me following my personal decision to swallow my pride and continue working. I needed the job; it paid well enough to get me through seminary without obligating Janice to work even though she chose to do so. Nevertheless, that was my commitment to her, so I merely shook my head as I walked back into the store, knowing that I had been ushered into corporate America as a good black man with a beard, and not as a qualified person for the job. I also became aware that I was being watched more closely than the other employees, which began to make me paranoid. So I kept a paper trail on everything I did, making sure that I could account for every dime and every minute of my working day. I knew that I had to watch my own back because I was a suspect for no reason other than my race.

I was definitely a hard worker, a characteristic that I had developed in Deer Path, and that was shaped even more while I was in the air force. I had been taught to do quality work or no work at all; I would even say I always strove for perfection. This was the way it was in the air force. My mistake was in believing when I got out that everyone viewed work performance the same. To my surprise, at Walden's my work ethic was taken as arrogance and bossiness. I had to literally learn a new language to get along with my co-workers there. Really, all I wanted to do was my job, but the other employees took my serious-ness as an insult. I couldn't figure it out. The employees wanted to goof off on the phone or talk for hours to their friends in the store, but as a manager, it was my job to accomplish certain goals nightly, and I needed the cooperation of the entire staff to do this.

Sometimes it just didn't seem that things would ever work out. Instead of cooperating with me, the employees would goof around when Mr. White left the store, leaving the bulk of the responsibility to me. Usually, the work got done, but only after I pushed and threat-ened. Never able to just be friendly or amicable with the store staff, I always had to get tough, and if I didn't, our tasks would not be com-pleted. As a result, I was made out to be the bad guy.

Another thing that bothered me was the disrespectful way Mr. White treated the employees, something I never did. I remember him saying, "Mr. Johnson, we need people who are going nowhere in life to work at our store. We give them a sense of purpose, and in return they give us their loyalty. Basically, Mr. Johnson, most of these people are going no further than where you see them today." I guess I was offended a little, but there was some truth to what he said. That was no reason, however, for him to treat the employees like second-rate citi-zens, kindred to small children or pets.

I figured that if I treated them fairly and with respect that the favor would be returned. Not so. Giving them all the respect in the world, I was still never able to get the crew at Walden's to work for me the way they worked for Mr. White, and I found that most of the time the employees, including the black ones, had a problem with a black per-son being their boss.

Mr. White's managerial approach astounded me. He would often call his white female workers degrading names. One of these ladies—Sue was her name—was extremely overweight and always crying on Mr. White's shoulder about some problem she was having at home.

He would always listen and appear to really care about her situation, so a bond grew between them, one of mutual dependency as well as mistrust of everyone else in management positions, including me. This, among other things, made Sue a thorn in my side.

Sometimes Sue's work areas needed straightening, but rather than tending to them, she overlooked them, preferring instead to talk on the phone or gossip with customers. She would seldom act this way when Mr. White was around because he would walk right up to her and say, "Get your fat a _ _ off of that phone and clean that damned aisle up." With a jovial response, Sue would run to her work area to clean and straighten it. I found it very interesting that most of the employees found his vulgar communication style inspiring and funny, except me.

I often heard him call women in the store fat a _ _, white trash, or slut, and they never reported him for it. Instead, they allowed themselves to be treated like animals. Mr. White had license with the staff that I knew could never have. If I were to ever call a white female employee the names Mr. White called them, I would have been sued and hanged on a tree. The humor in this whole scenario is that Sue purposely ignored me when I treated her with respect. She would often report me to Mr. White for merely asking her nicely to do her job. One day when I walked into the store, Mr. White stopped me and asked me to follow him to the back. Fortunately, I had gotten used to the storeroom conferences by then.

"Mr. Johnson, I have been having a few complaints about the way you communicate with the employees. They say you're too demanding."

Before I could even open my mouth in defense, he stopped me.

"Mr. Johnson," he continued, "Sue's husband was a Klansman. She's the one complaining about you the most."

I am thinking to myself, "What in God's name is he telling me this for? I don't care about her ex-hooded husband."

"Mr. Johnson, Sue has a hard time with you being a black man, and even a harder time with you as her boss. As a matter of fact, a lot of the employees are having a hard time with you being their boss."

I knew for sure that I was at my boiling point, but I wasn't ready to blow, so I just continued to listen. Then he said,

"Mr. Johnson, I have your back. When I am not here they know that you are in charge, and when you tell them to do something they are to do it whether you are blue or black. You are my voice when I am not here. I have explained this, especially to Sue. I told her to stop coming to me with petty s _ _ _. If she did her job you wouldn't have to tell her to do it."

Somehow that gave me some solace, but I wasn't completely sure that Mr. White believed what he was telling me because he would always pull employees to the side behind my back to question them about my shifts, which, in my eyes, dropped his credibility to the level of crap on the side of a trashcan. Again, my blackness seemed to be the center for many of the complaints by the white employees. Really, I began to get tired of it all. I couldn't even concentrate on my job fully because I began to worry that Sue's husband and his hooded friends might kidnap me one night to hang me on a rope. It got real stressful, but I kept doing the job because we needed the money.

One last incident became the impetus for my desire to leave Walden's. After coming in to report for a shift during the weekday, Mr. White flagged me down to show me something.

"Mr. Johnson, see those roughneck black kids walking down the aisle?"

"Yes," I replied, although disagreeing with his description of them.

"Those kids are trouble. They always steal from the candy aisle."

"Have you ever caught them stealing, Mr. White?" I asked.

"No, Mr. Johnson we haven't, but I know they have because Sue has told me that she has seen them do it." Like her word had any credibility with me anyway. This woman was married to a Klansman, for crying out loud.

He continued, "Mr. Johnson I want you to keep an eye on them. Maybe you can do something with them."

At once I began to think, "Who's to say that Sue is not stealing the candy and using the black kids as a cover-up?" The whole feel of the situation made my skin crawl. I felt belittled and angry over the wrongful accusation placed on the kids.

Many white people have an uncanny way of placing all blacks in the same group. They seem to feel that our blackness makes us monolithic. Among blacks, however, there are various social, religious, economic, and cultural milieus. Although our color bonds us as a result of our common history of slavery and injustice in the United States, it doesn't guarantee that all blacks can relate to one other socially. The color of our skin does not give us any more credibility with one another than it does with a white person.

After listening to this obviously ignorant phobic stereotype, I felt obligated to side with the kids. I had the desire to know them and befriend them, not because they were accused as thieves, but because, based on their color, they were misunderstood as human beings. I felt they needed a fair shake by someone in authority.

I walked from Mr. White's office to the candy aisle where the kids were. When I turned the corner, they immediately looked up at me and greeted me. One of them said, "Whas up!" I answered, "Whas up, little brothas." It felt good to hear the vernacular I had grown up with. It united us. One of the kids asked if I worked at the store. The answer was obvious because I was wearing a uniform, so the question was more one of surprise because these kids probably had never seen a black manager before. After a brief conversation with them, I found that the so-called rough necks were no more than young kids who liked to play in the candy and toy aisles, as any normal kid would do.

I began to work with that group often, giving them treats in the store when they brought their report cards to me. My relationship with them enabled me to see that I had an interest in youth and in justice, for it had hurt me so to see a group of black boys targeted for slander and abuse. I knew then that I would eventually commit much of my life to kids and to the inner city. I didn't know how, but I knew I would do it some day.

It occurred to me that black children, especially boys, are born into a more challenging set of circumstances than any other group in the

United States of America. Mainstream white Americans have placed all of our black children in the same boat. I thought that day that if our children were ever going to have a better chance at succeeding in life, it would be through the positive influence and mentorship of successful African American men and women. I had worked with youth at Friendship Baptist Church in Anchorage, and loved it, but I had never considered working with youth fulltime, let alone being one of those influential role models. After all, I was just a manager at Walden's. Somehow, working with the boys at the store pushed me further into making a decision that would change my life once more. Racial profiling had targeted these boys for evil, but God was turning the experience into good.

Chapter 27

"Though seeing, they do not see; though hearing, they do not hear or understand." Matthew 13:13

Seminary

My first semester at Southern was very difficult and challenging. I was learning new concepts and ideologies that were completely foreign to me.

It took me the entire fall semester of 1992 and winter term of 1993 to finally adjust to theological academia, quickly familiarizing myself with such concepts as ecclesiology, theodicy, existentialism, post-modernism, conservatism, liberalism, humanism, and a variety of others. I felt like someone literally stretched my brain during my first semester. I had had no idea that seminary would be such an intense cerebral endeavor.

For some reason, I thought we'd be reading a lot of scripture, praying, and helping one another along the ministerial path. Of course, this was not the case at all. My whole world of spirituality and intellectual capacity was challenged and rearranged. Everything that I thought I knew about God was scrutinized. This was probably the very thing Reverend Davis had tried to warn me about: exposure. Things had been simple at Friendship Baptist where I learned what Reverend Davis taught. On the other hand, at seminary I was exposed to a myriad of teachings, and it was quite refreshing. I was also introduced to a variety of ministry opportunities, whereas in Anchorage, I had figured that pastoring was the only viable ministry position. Now I was learning that ministers could go on the mission field, and into teaching, youth ministry, pastoral counseling, and a variety of consulting fields. The "call" was so much bigger than I had understood it previously that it was almost overwhelming. Simply put, seminary was an entirely new world of enlightenment, and I knew in my heart that I was growing and being prepared for the real world of theological endeavors. In Anchorage, I would have never had this opportunity. Coming to this realization confirmed my decision to pursue further training, and I was glad to be enrolled at Southern Baptist Theological Seminary.

My first introductory class was a colloquium consisting entirely of first semester students and designed to help us adjust to the newness of theological pursuits. I had a lot of fun in this class and met several people that would help shape my perspective on the world. Will, one of those people, was one of the few blacks that attended Southern. Because I was not only a racial minority there, but also a cultural minority—as a Northerner in the South and at a seminary that was completely permeated by Southern culture—I was thrilled to meet Will, thinking that he and I shared some commonality. In time, however, I would discover that though we were both black, Will and I were from two different worlds, and that difference would eventually separate us.

Will and another friend, Truman, introduced me to other brothas and sistas at Southern. Usually between classes, a good number of the black students would congregate in the Honeycutt Center, where many great conversations and debates took place. I was very impressed with the intellectual capacity of my fellow brothers and sisters, most of whom were much older than I and overflowing with sound wisdom. In the center, we discussed and analyzed class lectures during the meeting of the minds, and I learned more in those dialogues than I ever did in class. This precious time with my peers was the single most important facet of my growth at Southern. Unfortunately, however, many of us had trouble controlling our egos and pride, which usually led to conflict and someone always feeling a need to be the authority on some subject. As a result, many of my relationships were shallow, and I made very few friends at seminary, but the friendships that I did develop are still intact.

What disillusioned me most about Southern was the political conflict that existed in the Southern Baptist Convention, about which I had been totally naïve. Not only was this the nastiest conflict of ideologies that I had ever experienced, it was also my first experience with political turmoil in a religious setting. During my first year at Southern, the moderates primarily controlled the academic direction of the school. Yet, the conservatives were in the majority in the convention, which led to a tremendous amount of conflict within the convention and the seminary. This is important to note because the seminary was supported by the convention. Whenever money is connected to something, I have found that conflict is inevitable because someone will want control, and this is exactly what happened at the seminary.

By my second year at Southern, the conservatives finally positioned themselves at the school to appoint a conservative president. This would change the intellectual direction of the seminary. Eventually this also led to several sit-ins and student protests. The liberals and moderates knew that the new president was going to make major changes to align the school with the ideology of the convention, so many professors decided to resign before receiving their marching papers. It was a sad witness for new students and young Christians to see such a bitter and heartless battle among so-called mature, Christian leaders. I tried to stay out of the battle by focusing on my schoolwork, but this was hard to do with the professors becoming emotional and expressing their feelings in class. Many times, our classes turned into a gripe sessions for the Southern Baptist family. For the most part, the black students at Southern were on the outside of the fight and were therefore able to focus on our goals much better than many of our white peers. We simply didn't have the historical and emotional link to the Southern Baptist family that they had.

The Southern Baptist denomination was founded as a result of a Southern Baptist missionary's stance on slavery. In the mid-1800s, there was only one Baptist convention, but when the North and South began to differ on the issue of slavery, the Southerners decided to form a new convention that would permit and justify the ownership of slaves. Having had no idea prior to attending Southern that the past seminary leadership had theologically supported the institution of slavery, I was so appalled when I was informed of this in a history class that I wanted to leave the school, but this was not possible, so I stayed. Of course, the position of the school had changed by the time I arrived more than one hundred years later. But the fact remained that the institution of Southern was born on the back of my ancestors, literally.

It was due to this history that many of the blacks that attended Southern were mostly there only for an affordable theological education. The political fights and the emotional trauma that the white students experienced were simply not our issues. One brother told me, "Nev, the chicken has come home to roost." After coming to grips with the historical background of the seminary, I was in complete agreement with his statement. What the administration and students were experiencing was only what they had sown for generations. I was learning more than theology at seminary; I was learning about politics too.

As difficult as it was, I was able to adjust to the political baggage, but I never did quite adjust to my uniqueness among the other black students. The fact of the matter was that I was very different from the average seminarian, black or white, many of whom had experienced church work or church work and the black church tradition, which I had not. My experience had been more eclectic, and after being around my peers for a while the differences between us became more apparent, which caused me to become insecure. After all, I had tried so hard in the white world to prove myself, and now I was having to prove myself in the black church—an awfully frustrating situation. It was much later that I would understand that God had created me to do something different and unique with my eclectic experience with the world and the church and that I would to do things that my peers had neither the experience nor background to do.

I developed some good relationships with a variety of my seminary professors, among them the tall and distinguished looking Dr. Thomas Johnson, professor of social work, and one of two black faculty members at Southern. "Dad," as I called him, became my mentor and surrogate father. It was easy to claim him because we had the same last name. Like me, Johnson also struggled with racism at Southern. During the political transition there he was treated in a very unchristian manner, which I witnessed. Ultimately, he was hired by another school, and is now doing extremely well.

Johnson toughened me up in certain areas, especially leadership, and guided me through many a rough spots. He became my role model as I watched how he handled racism and leadership issues, doing everything completely by the book and professionally and never allowing the injustice of his treatment to push him into doing something that would injure his reputation.

Dr. Derrick Sanders was another one of my professor friends. Dr. Sanders had just graduated from a seminary in New York and had been hired as the new professor of ethics at Southern during my second year there. Since I was very interested in ethics, we developed a good friendship. He even helped me improve my writing skills. Dr. Sanders was always interested in the plight of Black America though he was ignorant to the inner city issues, such as drugs and violence. So I enlightened him by sharing my background and knowledge of these things and told him about my work experiences and confrontations with prejudice, and he sharpened my thinking with his keen intellect and deep passion for social justice.

There were many more professors that I befriended during my three-year tenure at Southern, all of whom influenced my theological perspective. When I left seminary after graduation in May 1995, I felt prepared for the world with my global theology and personal philosophy in hand and heart, all neatly packaged and ready to be spread. I was prepared for whatever life threw my way; after all, I was a trained theologian.

Chapter 28

"...and who knows but that you have come to royal position for such a time as this?" Esther 4:14

Teen Life

I worked at Walden's for about ten months. I aggressively learned the job in order to remain competent and to compete with my peers, and quickly accelerated past them. This is just how I wanted it to be because I knew from my past experiences that, being negatively stereotyped, I had to be the best. Sometimes this worked in my favor, giving me the extra fire I needed to excel.

I tolerated Walden's daily because I needed a job, but in my heart I wanted to work in the ministry, though I didn't know how it would happen. Friendship Baptist was the only place I had ever done any ministry, so I prayed and prayed like never before, hoping that God would hear my cry. Little did I know that God was about to open the door for my passion.

In January 1993, I met a young man named Jonathan who approached me on campus in the Honeycutt Center after hearing me speak to a group about my desire to start an urban ministry in the inner city. He immediately introduced himself to me, and then asked me if I had ever heard of Teen Life? I told him no. In fact, few of the blacks at the seminary had heard about Teen Life. After doing some research, I found that the group was a Christian, evangelical, youth organization, catering mostly to white middle-class teenagers. There was a chapter in Louisville, which happened to have an outreach to inner city youth which Jonathan directed. He was looking for someone to take his place, and had sought out me and a few others for this purpose. I was instantly interested ready to jump head first into this ministry without even hearing about the details. My excitement overruled my intellect, and I told Jonathan that I would follow-up on the position within two weeks.

Soon thereafter, I was hired by Teen Life, probably on the strength of my attending a conservative, evangelical seminary, since I had never before actually worked with evangelical Christians. My entrance into this most unique culture would be through Teen Life, which was staffed by people who had had very limited interaction with the people they were trying to serve—minorities and the poor. Considering just this fact, I wondered why they wanted to fund a ministry to black kids whom they most likely would never meet. Yet, they had significant enough interest in black kids and their salvation to pursue the endeavor, so I was hired to work with a population that most of them feared, and I was proud to do it. I was ignorant of the implications of their fear until much later in my career.

Unlike my structured nine to five job at Walden's, working for Teen Life was unpredictable. It was casual, less structured, undefined, and many times unprofessional. I was privileged to have the position, but at the same time, I felt that I had no support. No one seemed to know what I was supposed to do. Jonathan had already shipped out of Louisville, so I didn't even have him to lean on. I was left with nothing but a few kids and a couple of angry adult volunteers until my formal initiation, which took place at a board meeting.

I had never attended any type of board meeting before, so I tried draw a parallel between the experience and something in my past. In the military, the various departments wrote reports for the commander or section supervisors and presented them at staff meetings. After asking Chad, my boss, about Teen Life protocol, he concluded that writing a report would be a great idea. I spent an entire weekend on the report to impress the board with my ability to do the job. I had to prove myself in any job, but also—like it or not—I had the extra burden of representing my people.

Chad, who was the board director, gave me directions to the board member's house where the meeting was to be held. I thought to myself how unlike the business world it was to meet in someone's home instead of in an office. Like most suburban communities in Louisville, this one was totally unfamiliar to me, and as I followed Chad's directions, I could see that I was driving into an exclusive neighborhood where the homes sat on top of hills, and the garages were bigger than my apartment. I knew right away that I was going to be working with very successful business people, which made me even more nervous about my presentation. Flabbergasted by the wealth of the community, the only thing that I could compare with it was White Hills in East Lansing.

I parked near the sidewalk and walked up a steep hill towards the door, passing by BMWs, Mercedes Benzes, Jeeps, and Cadillacs in the driveway, which was further confirmation that these board members brought home above average salaries. As I approached the door I was once again awed at the size and upkeep of this place. Trying to remain calm and collected, I knocked on the door, and within seconds a white woman, seeming a little hesitant at first, opened it and welcomed me in with a smile. "You must be Nevlynn," she said. "Yes, I am," I replied

"Hello. My name is Donna Riser. Welcome to our home. The board meeting will be held in the entertainment room," she said. I was immediately impressed. These people had an entertainment room. That was cool to me. My entertainment room was the hard and cold cement floor in the basement on Eldridge. Once I entered the Riser home, the board members greeted me, and I continued to meet more of them as they arrived over the next fifteen minutes.

Once everyone was gathered, the meeting officially started with a prayer and a devotion from scripture. Chad, who had hired me, sat next to me and introduced me as the new part-time urban director. The board members seemed to be excited about me and the future of the urban ministry, which led to an array of questions. First, they wanted to hear my testimony, including how I came to know the Lord, my family background, and my previous work experience. After sharing this information with them, I gave the formal report I had written about my goals for the urban ministry. They were shocked that I was prepared to report on the ministry so soon, and Chad told me afterwards what a good impression I had made on them. It seemed as though I was off to a good start.

I learned one important bit of information that night: the board members were seriously committed to this Teen Life ministry, in part because it had transformed some of their children's lives. Hence, they wanted nothing more than for other teens to experience the same transformation.

My Teen Life budget was well over $150,000. I had heard of many fundraisers, including those for the local NAACP and Urban League, both of which support economic growth and legal representation for minorities. But I had never heard of an organization for teenagers in the black community with the structure and financial support of Teen Life.

There were no more than twelve people on the board and over half of the budget was already committed by them. It simply amazed me that a small group of wealthy Christians was able to align itself in support of a budget of such enormity and quietly touch the lives of hundreds of high school teenagers. I later found that small groups like this one were spread throughout the world through Teen Life, a multi-million dollar, international, high school-based, Christian ministry. When I realized the group's magnitude, I began to think that I was in way over my head, and I felt a strong urge to leave and find a part-time position at a black church. Even though I was not as knowledgeable about the black church experience as some of my seminary classmates, I was at least black. This fact alone affirmed my notion that it would be better for me to work with black people than white ones, but I remained on staff, probably because I realized that there were endless possibilities for ministry in the city. Teen Life seemed to have the passion for kids to know Jesus as well as the resources to make it happen. I thought this just might be my unique niche.

By my fifth month as a Teen Life staff member, I had developed a rapport with many of the kids in the Louisville West End section. My heart went out in particular to fatherless teenagers. Because I had felt the pain of not having a father I knew that if I could do nothing else, I could relate to fatherless teens. Word spread quickly about the ministry, and soon vanloads of kids were visiting our outreach weekly. A lot of them lived in the projects, and even more were coming from broken homes. The programming at Teen Life was fun, and the message was very Christ-centered, but the kids really came around for the relationships. It seemed that they loved to have things revolve around their world, and Teen Life did this best. Mostly, they felt wanted and safe. It was the one time in the week that many inner city teenagers were able to be young and free.

It was hard for me to turn off the needs of a hurting group of people, especially kids, and I soon fell in love with my new calling and responsibilities. The array of issues that many of the kids experienced was so close to my heart. Like so many of them, I had had no one in my life to give me sober direction except my mom, so I tried to be to them what I, myself, had missed during my high school years. As a result, my work hours got later, and my commitment grew stronger. My education became more meaningful, as well, because working with complex inner city issues enabled me to challenge the privileged white theology that was taught at Southern. Much of what I had learned was theoretical, but my work demanded a practical theology. To this day I believe the poor and the underprivileged kept me real to the game. Dr. Sanders, and especially Dr. Johnson, were real advocates during this time. As I struggled with Southern Baptist theology, they were able to help me translate theory into practice. At the same time, I began to read works by James Cone, Cornell West, Major Jones, Martin Luther King Jr., Gayraud Wilmore, J. Deotis Roberts, and several other black theologians. It became clear to me that the kids I worked with needed to hear about a God who suffered, was born in a ghetto, and went homeless. So black and liberation theology definitely helped shape my ideas and practice.

What began as a part-time job turned into a full-time passion. Days on the job ran into nights in order to keep pace with my enormous desire to change the world for so many hurting kids. At least once a week I returned home well after midnight.

Chapter 29

"…this is the Lord's doing; it is marvelous in our eyes."
Psalm 118:23

A NEW BIRTH

I remember the day when my wife told me it was time for our baby to be born. She was ready, and it seemed from her labor pains that the baby was ready too. We were living in Louisville, attending school—I was at Southern seminary and she, at a local university working on her degree in social work. It was our first year in Louisville, and once again we found ourselves facing a new challenge—preparing to raise a child.

I was studying when she interrupted me with, "Nevlynn, it's time to go to the hospital." I put my books down and ran for the video-recorder to start taping. While I was videotaping, Janice was calling the doctor, who told her to check into the hospital. Minutes later we were grabbing our bags and miscellaneous items, headed in that direction. All the while, I was trying to record everything. Anyone looking on would have been amused to see so many things going on at once. But unbelievably, Janice was calmer than I was, so there wasn't too much stress.

When we got to the hospital, we were checked into a temporary room where we didn't have to stay too long before our doctor arrived. Janice's water hadn't broken, so the doctor induced her labor. Minutes later, she began to have painful contractions. I continued to film the entire episode. When the pains got too much to bear, Janice demanded that I turn the camera off. I was a bit disillusioned because I was really getting into the filming of the whole thing, but I put the camera down and walked near her to console her. When I reached for her, she asked me not to touch her. She was hurting a lot, and I couldn't relate. All I could do was stand there and try to be supportive. Watching her go through the birthing process made me feel completely helpless because there was nothing I could do to console her.

To complicate matters, the baby's head was too big for normal delivery, so the doctor decided to give Janice a Cesaraen, and within seconds after being administered anesthesia, she was barely conscious. When the doctor made the incision in Janice, I felt sick and like I needed some of that anesthesia; it seemed that blood was everywhere and that I could feel the cut in my abdominal area.

I didn't pass out, though, the way I've heard that so many fathers do. Instead, I handled the situation by watching every move, and listening to every word spoken by the doctor. If Janice was out of it, I would be there to make sure things went okay. Barely able to speak, she whispered weakly, "How are things going?" With a green face, I turned to her and tried to persuade her that everything was going well. Before she could respond, I turned back just in time to see the doctor pull the baby out of her abdomen.

My son entered the world. I didn't know what to do when I saw him. Tears filled my eyes and my heartbeat increased when I saw Nevlynn II in the hands of the nurse, and I was absolutely speechless. I watched her wash him off and put a little knitted cap on his head. Then she placed Nevlynn in my arms, making me the second person after herself to hold him. I was awe struck looking at the most wonderful creation of God, our son, as he was snuggled in my arms. I rocked him and watched him try to open his little eyes. I whispered in his ear, "My son, may the creator of earth and heaven lead you and guide you all the days of your life." Then I thanked God Almighty for the blessing of a child to nurture, rear, and teach.

Caught up in the miracle of birth, I had almost forgotten Janice lying there, but she got my attention as she struggled to turn her head towards the baby and me. She smiled at me after looking at little Nevlynn, and I reached down and slowly placed him on her chest. She carefully placed her arms around him and gently hugged him. I could tell that she was so happy, but she also was very tired, so I took the baby from my drowsy wife, and walking down the hall more cautiously than I had ever walked anywhere before, I went into the nursery to place our son in his cradle. Outside the nursery, my mother stood in the baby window waiting to see him, and when the nurse lifted him from my arms and held him for her to see, a quick glance at Mom told me that she was a very proud grandmother. It was time to go back to check on my wife, but not before I saw the nurse tag little Nevlynn with his identification bracelet.

I moved back to the delivery room, quietly and fearfully watching the doctor stitch Janice's abdomen back together. She had lost a lot of blood by the time her stitching was complete, and her skin looked pale and gray. I was scared. For a moment, I didn't know if she was going to make it. All I could do was just stay by her side and pray.

While I was waiting for her to recover, I realized for the first time that women actually risk their lives giving birth. This realization gave me a new level of appreciation for all mothers and a new awareness that the very act of child delivery is a gift to humanity that no one could ever repay. For two nights I prayed fervently for Janice to be healed and restored, and by the grace of God, she was.

It felt good to have my new son and wife together with me. Janice and I managed to do it, I thought. We started a family. I was committed to my family, but especially to my son that he would never have to go through life wondering who his father was. I would always be there for him!

Chapter 30

"...but time and chance happen to them all." Ecclesiastes 9:11

Curve Ball

I have never been a real baseball fan. As a matter of fact, after being smashed in the head once with a baseball flying at sixty miles per hour, I decided to never walk anywhere near a bat, field, or baseball, though some time later I did attend a few games, but very few. What has fascinated me the most about baseball is the advantage of the pitcher, who has the unique ability to control the game—if he is good enough—whereas, the batter stands holding his bat, not knowing what throw is coming his way, but always having to be prepared for it. Because of this disadvantage, many batters have walked off the field horribly disappointed that they struck out. Many times, they were thrown a curve ball, and that was all she wrote. "If I had only seen it coming," I'll bet they've often said.

A curve ball is the best way to explain what happened next in my life. I was ready to bat, but I kept missing the ball. The pitcher of life threw me a curve, and I didn't see it coming. At least I don't think I saw it coming. Regardless, I missed.

After the baby was born, the roles in our marriage changed. Suddenly, Janice was faced with being a full-time mom, at least for a couple of years, and I was faced with finding full-time employment to support our family. I had just completed my first year at seminary with two long years left to go, and was working two part-time jobs on campus, and doing Teen Life. Janice was unemployed and a full-time student and a full-time mom—if that is possible. Our schedules were maxed out. Had it not been for my mother's help, life would have been most impossible.

Before Nevlynn was born, Janice and I never discussed who would be responsible for what. I assumed, wrongly, that Janice would accept the responsibility of being a homemaker and a full-time mom, at least until our son was able to talk—an assumption that caused much friction for two years and began a series of difficulties that I am still unable to clearly articulate.

When I graduated from seminary in 1995, the next challenge was to find full-time employment. Teen Life had asked me to come on full time and after several months of praying, I had agreed to accept the offer. Janice understood that my responsibilities would increase, but neither of us knew what that really looked like. At the same time, Janice began graduate work at another university.

I couldn't conceive of my responsibilities increasing the way they did. All of a sudden I was not only working with teenagers, but I was fundraising, developing committees, involved in a building project, setting up community-awareness projects, and meeting with the power hitters of the city. On any given day, I would dress in a suit that morning to meet with a millionaire who might give money to our outreach program, and by evening I would have changed into my blue jeans to hang out with the roughest of the rough teenagers. I was wearing many hats at once, and it was very tiring, yet exciting at the same time.

The only reason I kept at it was because of my calling in ministry and my commitment to the kids. I knew they needed to understand the Christian life, and they had to have a safe place to hang out. The only way these things would happen was for Teen Lifers to get out there and expose ourselves in ministry. There was one problem, however. I felt very unsupported by the Teel Life board of directors. They would say that they supported my efforts, but the money was always slow in coming. It seemed as though I was always justifying the needs of inner city ministry to suburban white people. It became a real burden. For years Teen Life had only reached out to suburban white teenagers whose needs were so different than inner city kids' needs. To compound my disappointment, turning to black churches for help was even more frustrating. Usually, they would put me off because I was seen as a representative of a white, paternalistic organization. My race and commitment to the community didn't even make a difference to them.

The tremendous economic and social disparity between the inner city and the suburbs necessitated a holistic approach to the outreach ministry, but many board members were uncomfortable with this method. "What are we, some social agency or something?" board members would scornfully ask. Over and over again I was hitting my head against a wall and felt smothered by tradition and ignorance. I began to think that my time at Teen Life was up after working hard and endlessly full time for two years, and achieving only a few milestones. I concluded that Teen Life was simply too narrow-minded to grow and change.

I am sure that my frustration affected Janice since she was the only one I could talk to about my struggles. I know that she watched me work many days and many nights trying to make a difference, without much appreciation from Teen Life for my efforts. So, after a four-year stalemate in Louisville (two years part time, and two years full time), I was determined to leave Teen Life. I thought about becoming a pastor, but I knew that would be even more demanding on my family and me. Stumped for ideas, I began to think about other cities where I could get better support for inner city ministry.

In the winter of 1996, I met with my regional director to talk about some options, and Houston, Texas, came to the top of the list. I had lived in Houston before, and I felt sure that the resources were there to develop solid inner city ministries. Before I could make my request, however, the director offered me an opportunity in Memphis, Tennessee. Of the many cities that went through my mind as I was thinking about moving, Memphis was never one of them. But after realizing how serious he was, I decided to talk to my wife about it. Janice agreed for us to take a look at the opportunity.

Months later in Memphis, a number of seemingly nice people interviewed Janice and me (another caveat of evangelical ministries—usually the wife and husband are interviewed). The board there appeared to be well structured and focused, too. I was so impressed with everything that I was wooed into the city of Memphis, thinking it would certainly be our next and final stop. We would raise our family in Memphis, I thought to myself. After a few more visits and interviews, I was offered the position on Christmas Eve, 1996. What a wonderful gift, I thought, and just in time for Christmas and the new year.

Things seemed to fall into place like the pieces of a puzzle. Janice and I quickly found a house in a great community; she also found a position at a church working with teenagers, and our son was enrolled at its private school. The only problem was that I had to commute for three months before I could move. So Janice and our son moved to Memphis ahead of me. Things really seemed to be working out for the better, at least until I joined Janice and Nevlynn. Then, for reasons that I could not understand, my relationship with Janice became strained, and for the entire year of 1997, she and I had a lot of ups and downs. But, in my mind, things were not so far gone that I thought divorce was on the horizon.

The curve ball came one day in early March of 1998. On that fateful day, I walked into the house after work and found Janice calmly sitting on the couch. I smiled at her, and she smiled back.

"Hey, what's up darlin?" I said.

"Nevlynn, I need to talk to you about something," she replied.

The inflection in her tone let me know that something bad was about to happen, and I got butterflies in my stomach. But overall, Janice seemed calm, and with apparently little emotion, she began to speak.

"Nevlynn, a lot of things have happened since we've been married," she started. "I have felt pushed to be someone I am not. The roles and the pressure to be your wife have been hard, and I have felt like I've lost my identity. I am tired of being someone that I am not; I want to be me all the time."

I am thinking, *What in the world is she talking about? Loss of identity? Playing roles?*

She continued, "Nevlynn, I don't want to be married anymore. I want a divorce, and I have made preparations to move out soon."

I just looked at her at first, and then I realized that she was serious. Suddenly and unexpectedly, tears welled up in my eyes, and before I knew it I was crying. As much as I wanted to deny what was happening, I couldn't. It was hard to believe that my wife was saying she wanted out of the marriage. I couldn't process this unwelcome information. She simply didn't want to be married anymore? Things were definitely falling apart, and I had no control over them.

By this time my son was four years old and was about to graduate from pre-kindergarten. Unlike me, he had had a loving mother and father, so I began to think how he would respond to the news that his mommy and daddy were separating. I wouldn't be able to tuck him into bed every night. Custody issues would have to be worked out. It was all too hard for me to bear. I began to weep like a child. I felt hurt and betrayed. I wanted to pinch myself. Surely this was a nightmare. Janice wanted out of the marriage, and she was serious! Within minutes my whole life was out of control, and I began to feel that I had no reason to live.

I walked out of the door still crying, and opening the door to my car, I sped off with thoughts about killing myself. Every time I approached another car, I thought about smashing mine into it, but I couldn't. I couldn't even run off the road at high speed into a ditch. A force, it seemed, was holding me, and keeping me from doing what my mind kept suggesting. Thoughts of suicide competed with images of my son without a father, and I realized that only a punk would take his life because he wasn't man enough to deal with this issue. My son didn't need to pay for something that he didn't create, my better mind told me.

After driving and struggling with my thoughts for miles, I decided to stop and rest a while, and by the grace of God, I was at a lake. Peaceful and calming, it seemed to invite me to roll down the car window, take a deep breath, and recline my seat. Then quietly, I began to truly think about my life.

What had gone wrong? Was this something God had planned? None of it made sense. The worst part about it was that I had no power to change the direction in which my marriage was going. I loved Janice, but there seemed to be little I could do to make things right. I was at an all-time low. Everything I believed in, everything I put my trust in, was all up in the air now, and I had no idea where life was going to lead me. In fact, life as I had known it for nine years was over. My marriage was over too. The very idea of divorce went against the grain of everything I believed in as a Christian.

The lake had helped me think some, but I hadn't come up with any answers there. When I got back home, I still felt that my manhood and identity had been challenged in unspeakable ways, and I slumped into overpowering feelings of worthlessness, uselessness, and abandonment. Within hours of Janice's awful announcement of divorce, I had fallen into a deep depression, and for the first time in my life, I experienced complete and utter confusion about everything, and could barely make even the smallest decisions. One day I would think one way about a situation; the next day I would feel another way. I would wake up optimistic and go to bed pessimistic. Sunny days became dreary for me. Mostly, I just didn't want to get out of the bed to see or speak to anyone. But I had to. There were meetings and lunches to attend. There were teens to minister to. So I went through the paces with very few people around me even knowing what was going on. I had to maintain.

Chapter 31

"A man of many companions may come to ruin, but there is a friend who sticks closer than a brother." Proverbs 18:24

Friends

I never realized until my impending divorce how important relationships were. For the first time in my adult life, I was vulnerable, broken, and paralyzed, and I had to learn to depend on God's strength in ways than I never had before.

Anyone who was around me during my divorce would have said about my personality and character that I was a hard-working, self-sufficient guy. There is no question that I set the pace wherever I landed, and enjoyed getting the job done well and professionally. The sad part is that no one would have ever dreamed that I was a broken man, needing prayer, comfort, and encouragement. Still on the Teen Life staff, I just knew that this personal failure in my life would end my career in Christian ministry. My image as a black man, father, professional, and husband would be ruined, I thought, so I struggled to keep up my front.

Well, eventually I reached a point where I had to give up all of my self-sufficient, image-keeping stuff and just rely on the power of God to get me through. I remember sitting in a room by myself one day, wondering whom to call. All I wanted were answers from anyone, for it seemed that even God had abandoned me and was silent. As I was sitting there all alone, I began to think of all the people with whom I had developed relationships in my life, but out of all of them, I could only think of one person to call, and that was one of my mentors from Southern Seminary. Though he did help, he was far away. I needed somebody close by, and soon. I had gotten to a place where I no longer cared about my reputation and image. I was in survival mode. Any help would do. I turned to God and prayed for relief, and unbeknownst to me, He began answering my prayer by touching the hearts of a number of people concerning me.

As I began to reach out, sharing my dark story with people on my board and committee, and not knowing how they would respond, they began to support me like I had never been supported before. For the first time in my life, I genuinely felt that I was being ministered to, and surprisingly, by a group from which I least expected it. I just knew that people would turn their backs on me. But this special group of people, who happened to be white, took me into their lives as a true brother.

There were times that I felt as though I was literally adopted by families. I received cards in the mail. I was sent on retreats and to counselors. Most of the time, I went by myself because my wife was committed to the divorce. She was enjoying her new found freedom with so-called relatives and friends. Alone, I felt that I was riding solo on this one.

On the very day that Janice moved from our house, one man even came by and sat with me in the middle of floor until most of the house was empty. We didn't have a big conversation, either. He was merely committed to being present with a brother in time of need. However, at one point he helped Janice move some of her things out to the moving truck, and in the process, respectfully tried to talk to her about her choice, but she was unwilling to dialogue with him. My wife didn't want anything to do with me or anyone who opposed her decision. That was a rough day, but his presence was the most powerful thing I had experienced in a long while, and he was a white man.

Grace and mercy became embodied in flesh through many people as I became more and more vulnerable, but the fascinating factor in it all was that the people who stepped in the gap for me the most were white. Slowly but surely, the color of peoples' skin became of little or no concern to me. Each person who entered my life at that special time became ministers of mercy to me, and I will never forget them.

To this day I believe that God worked through several people to teach me a lot of lessons about grace, mercy, and relationship. Human beings are made for relationship, and it is so sad that race and culture separate us so in this country and world. I am just so glad that God sees through our insecurities, fears, and ignorance and becomes our strength in our weakness. He used my circumstance not only for me, but for others too. God's hands were on me, and He met me via a channel I would have least expected—people of another race and culture.

Don't get me wrong. I do believe that our society is still sick with the poison of racism, prejudice, and the color line. My situation doesn't nullify the continued injustices that African American people still endure to this day. Rather, my circumstance only created a level of consciousness that woke me up as an individual. I can no longer make assumptions that I can live without true friends, and that those friends can't be white. With God, all things are possible, even breaking through the walls of ignorance and pride, which, as Christians, we are often guilty of erecting.

Epilogue

"When I was a child, I talked like a child, I thought like a child, I reasoned like a child. When I became a man, I put childish ways behind me. Now we see but a poor reflection as in a mirror; then we shall see face to face. Now I know in part; then I shall know fully, even as I am fully known." **1 Corinthians 13:11-12**

You know, there have probably been quite a few spots that you, the reader, may have asked questions about. I would surmise that there are at least three areas in which you want resolution: my mother, my ex-wife, and me. The reason you do not already have these answers is due to my own process of introspection. It has taken me a while to really come to grips about all three issues, especially my ex-wife.

First, I would like to say that although my uncle was a male hero for me, in many ways, my mother was the bigger and more holistic hero. I literally watched her struggle to raise me and to keep her own sanity as a black woman, which I know could not have been easy.

My mother was the main reason that I was able to make it through some tough points in my life. She believed in me, and supported almost all of my decisions. I would say that she was and continues to be my cheerleader. It was my mother that helped to instill in me a work ethic. It was through her that I learned never to hit a woman. It was by the direction of my strong black mother that I learned that I was to treat people right, and to fight with my pen and not my fists. Though I used my fists sometimes, I recognized as I grew up how wise my mother's instruction was to me as it relates to communication and logic in human relations. My mother was my main teacher, and she was able to pull off the rearing of a black boy in a society that already

207

had me pegged out to be thug. Granted she made mistakes, but she gave me all that she could to make me into a good man; she did her best to point me towards God.

During most of my childhood, I don't remember my mother dating very much. From the age of five until my eighteenth birthday, to my knowledge my mother dated four or five guys. Two of these I do believe were very serious relationships, but she never gave me a lot of details about them. Nor did I want any information. My only concern was that my mother was happy, which for the most part, I don't believe that she was.

I must admit that I wanted some of the guys my mother dated to be my father—not so much due to their parenting skills, but because I wanted a consistent man in my life. I wanted her to have a husband, and I wanted a father. Many of my friends had a dad who was involved in their lives, even if he was divorced from their mothers. I had no one, and it got to me many times. This is probably the reason that I have such a strong and driving desire to be a good father. I want to be there for my son, always.

Not too long after my first marriage, my mother got married to a guy who had alcoholic and violent tendencies. Although she was a college graduate and a mental health professional, she was drawn to an unhealthy relationship. Within two to three years of marriage to this tyrant—ironically a man very similar to my grandfather—she separated from him and made up her mind that she would no longer allow herself to be abused by a man.

Soon thereafter, Mom moved to Louisville to be with me. In many ways, I became the center of her life again. For her it was okay, but in my opinion she didn't learn how to enjoy life apart from me, and now apart from her new grandson. In fact, she dedicated most of her life to me, giving up many of her own desires to ensure that I had the best that I possibly could. There were times that I wondered if she really cared about my personal welfare, but time has shown that she really did—even through my divorce.

My mother did what so many mothers, particularly black single mothers, do so well. She sacrificed for me to have a life that would be better than her own. She made decisions about our life to the best of her ability, and gave me the best that she could with what she had—and believe me, she did not have very much.

My mother is my true hero because she made something out of nothing, and I will never forget that. My life in many respects is a tribute to her, for if she hadn't made so many special sacrifices, my life would be totally different. I love her for that.

I'd say that it is now time for my mother to enjoy life. She was pushed to give to everyone else, but never accepted that life was created for her to enjoy and to be taken care of, too. I am happy to report that she is finding her way to a life of joy, peace, and purpose outside of her grandson and me. One day, I know she will write her story and it will be a bestseller because she is a true testimony of perseverance.

As for my divorce and my ex-wife, that whole situation was a trip. I don't think that I have ever in my life experienced as many emotions as I felt—and sometimes continue to feel—as a result of that event. Indeed, as I write these words, emotions rise in me that I thought were long gone.

I recognize that life can take some wild turns, but I never expected that my life would take the turn towards divorce. I remember how Janice changed when we got to the point of defining the specifics of the divorce settlement. At one point, she wanted only to have a new life of freedom and personal choice.

"I am a free spirit," is what she said to me during this settlement process.

"All I want to do is be ME all the time." Of course, listening to this diatribe, I was quietly thinking, *What exactly were you doing for nine years, pretending to be someone else?* How can a person pretend for nine years, and why would one do it? However, that is what seems to have happened. The whole marriage seemed to be a comedy routine with pretense for a script. Now all Janice wanted was a new life away from me and the many responsibilities that come with being married.

"All I want is out of this marriage. I don't want anything from you. I don't want the house; I was even told that I was entitled to half of your retirement, but I don't want it," she said.

First of all, I didn't even think of half of the things that she was discussing with me, being more concerned at the time about saving our family. Family was all that I had, so it seemed. My son, whom I would die for till this day, and my then wife, were my world. Why would I be thinking about assets? Everything that really mattered was slipping through the door. I had watched—feeling completely helpless and hopeless—as she moved my son and our furniture out of the house. And I learned the meaning of silence and loneliness from that time of emptiness.

Second, I thought that she would come back, so there would be no need to talk about details. Although she and I had discussed a few things, I avoided being serious about them. Instead, I was in complete denial for months until I finally realized that this was for real, and life was about to be very different than I had imagined.

What started out as "I don't want anything," turned into "I want everything I can get." I guess Janice's so-called friends and family coached her along the divorce process. It even got to the point of detailed issues regarding custody of our son. That completely upset me beyond mention. My son is my heart, and I could never imagine life without him.

The courts, in general, don't give a hoot about the dad. They simply see him as the provider only. As a man I felt like I was only seen as a dollar bill, not a father to my son. Had I had the money to push for full custody, I would have.

See, I realized quickly that lawyers are in the business for money, and in our culture, divorce is always sure money for them; they really don't even care who wins because they get paid either way. Divorce is about the hardest and most emotionally trying thing that a person can experience. It is like someone close to you dying, but the grieving process continues for a lifetime because the other person isn't dead. None of these emotional facts matter to lawyers, who deal with people in these vulnerable states all the time. Some lawyers—not all—will play on people's emotions if allowed to. As much as I wanted to get even with my ex, I knew that it would cost a lot of money to do so; my lawyer had let me know that up front.

In fact, my attorney was a woman who, herself, had been in a messed-up divorce. She even treated me like she was a little upset with me sometimes because of my uncertainty about how to approach the situation.

Lawyers want you to go in to win, so their share can be bigger, but they don't understand that while they see divorces every day and are jaundiced, you see a divorce perhaps once in a lifetime, and that is one time too many. You simply aren't in an emotional space to protect yourself or think clearly.

My lawyer had made up in her mind that if we were to win custody of my son, I would have to humiliate and destroy my ex. In court, we would have to attack Janice's character, her motherhood, and her ethics. Of course, this would only happen if I hired a private investigator, who in most cases would take anywhere from six months to a year to build a case, depending upon what my spouse was doing that was questionable.

After several visits and discussions with my attorney, I knew that

I would have to pay a private investigator for at least six months, pay the attorney for all of the legal work that she and her paralegal would do, and in addition pay court fees and copy fees, and for therapy sessions for my son, and so on. Even if I had gone to court and followed my attorney's suggestions, there was no certainty that I would even win the case.

"Mr. Johnson, we have a fifty-fifty chance," she said.

I was thinking, "It is not fifty-fifty with my money." It looked as if the court costs and legal fees, and other professional fees would have added up to well over fifteen to twenty thousand dollars—an amount of money I didn't have at the time.

Therefore, I took the high road by filing for a no-fault divorce, even though I knew there was something fishy going on. I just couldn't prove it. In addition, I wasn't prepared to take my son through any unnecessary changes. The separation and then the divorce were enough.

It became more important to me to just spend time with my son and come out of the whole thing with integrity and peace. And that is exactly what I did, even though I still ended up paying for the attorney, courts, and psychologist's fees.Further, I knew the courts weren't favorable towards men in custody cases anyway. I guess a lot of deadbeat men have made it tough for good dads to win in court.

There were times, I must admit, that I had some violently detailed fantasies about Janice, especially during or after I had spent a little time with my son. It seems that she always said something to provoke me when I would pick him up or take him home. I can't say how many days I thought of letting loose on her and everyone around her. It would have been easy. That is what my family background had taught me to do.

I had often heard of domestic violence situations during divorce that resulted in the death of at least one person, and can't say that something violent didn't go through my mind. It was natural, in some ways. Every time I saw Janice I thought of her betrayal, lies, and masks, and was offended at the very pit of my soul.

I would have to say it was my faith in the Lord that kept me from going off on her. Fortunately, I was placed in a unique community of Christian men and women, and I owed God, them, and the young people I worked with an example of forgiveness and peace. Now, I can't say that I had forgiven Janice for everything, but I did realize that life does, indeed, go on. She did what she had to do. My ex was convicted by her own inner struggles, and she made decisions based upon her own values and experience. And that's that; I will never be able to change the outcomes of her decision. So I had to deal with myself, and my faith and friends have helped me to do that in a variety of ways. I remember a phrase that got me through many a day from one of my mentors, the guy who sat in the middle of the floor with me the day my wife moved out.

"Nevlynn, whatever you do in this process, glorify God." I am thinking *glorify God. How in the heck can I glorify God in any of this mess?*

Well, those words from my mentor turned out to be one of the founding principles that I live by now. It is that principle that has enabled me to move on and pursue life like I have never done before. I still have my moments, but they are subject to my values and principles. Had I moved on my emotions, I know I would be in jail, dead— or even worse—in a psychiatric ward, confused and lonely.

So much has happened in my life during my thirty years. Some things I can understand, and even explain. Yet, there are far more things that I cannot understand or explain. Life has been one big roller coaster, and at most points I have felt like I was riding alone. Realistically, there is no way that I should be living, partly because I made some poor choices that could have caused a premature death. But many other things beyond my control were largely influenced by the mistakes and errors of the adults around me. By the grace of God, I made it through. I am here, I believe, because God has a plan for me.

The journey has not been easy; the road of life has been bumpy and challenging. Often in life we don't slow down enough to listen to the quiet whisper in our souls, and unfortunately, for some of us it takes a life-altering experience to hear that voice.

I could write in these last few pages how awful life has been, but that is not at all true. I have experienced some negative and positive things in life, but all of them have been for my good. I am a better man as a result of all the things that have happened. I try to accept everything as a lesson so I can continue in the developmental process of my faith walk. Without question, I could have avoided some negative experiences if I simply had known what to do, but many times I didn't. As a result, I learned by experience, which is the only teacher sometimes.

Life has not gotten easier, but it has gotten much clearer. While living in a broken world, surely we will all have challenges. Some of those challenges will take place in our families, our health, our businesses, our friendships, and, yes, even in our spirituality. But the good news is that we don't have to live a broken, defeated life. Every challenge that comes into our lives is to strengthen us as well as those who are in our circle of influence. In spite of the chaos and challenges in my life, I am still moving toward my dreams. None of these temporary things has taken me from my love and passion for life. As a matter of fact, I have a stronger desire for life now than ever before. Not only have I stopped to smell the roses, I have also taken the time to appreciate their beauty. I have so much to live for. Nothing has destroyed me; everything has made me better.

Now, I look to a wonderful future that God has planned for me. I can't change what happened yesterday, but I sure can change what life will be like for me tomorrow. I am finding my way, day by day, through the corridors of life, and this is rewarding and most gratifying. When it is all said and done, I want to live life to its fullest, and to do that I need faith, courage, and wisdom to appreciate the victories of yesterday and to face the challenges of tomorrow. This is my journey into manhood.

As I worked through the dark days of divorce and the shadows of my past, I began to write poetry and memoirs of my life's discoveries. I will end with one of these writings as my gift to all those brothers and sisters who experience the pain of loss and the joy of discovery. Peace be unto you!

The Finale

Somewhere along the way, I had a picture of joyful bliss and perfect days. My lack of wisdom and experience dictated those innocent thoughts, as well meaning as they were. But life has thrown me some blows, and reality has opened my eyes to see a whole new world of possibilities.

Never before have I understood life the way I do now.

Hurricanes destroy flourishing cities.
Leaves fall from perfectly healthy trees.
Birds drop from the sky without notice to their death.
Beautiful flowers wither, from the bottom to the top.
Sunny days turn to rain.
Special loved ones die.
Spouses walk away.
Cancer creeps into the cavity of the human body.
Loneliness catapults some into the darkness of depression.
Hunger rips away at the flesh of children.
Poverty pushes communities to hopelessness.
Substance abuse creates broken homes.
Wealth creates a false sense of security.
Violence cuts through the golden ribbon of peace.
Life simply is no fairy tale:
Cinderella doesn't always find her prince.

The sleeping beauty doesn't always wake up from the horror of darkness.
Snow White doesn't always find a community of purity.
The Beauty doesn't always change the Beast.
Goldilocks doesn't always get the chance to run away.
Nor does the great hunter always kill the dragon.
Such is life, I've learned.
Learn to live with the disappointments,
Learn to walk with the let downs,
We were never promised good times always.
But, good times do happen.
We must learn not to depend on the good times for our Joy.
If hope lies in perfection,
If our dreams are anchored in blissful times,
If our peace is rooted on a happy ending,
Surely, life will be hell!
God didn't intend it this way, but our broken world calls for it.
Jesus never promised to save us from the storms.
He didn't even promise to calm them.
Jesus promised to never forsake us.
Jesus promised to never leave us.
That's what we can all depend on, the presence of Jesus.
We must trust that as life changes, and we are faced with the raging seas, that the Lord will do what is sufficient for each of us.
And believe me, what is sufficient for one is not sufficient for another.
Somewhere along the way, my mind and my dreams have changed.
Life is truly a paradox; this I've learned to understand, even accept.
No longer will I have an answer for everything.

I will simply be content with the answers God gives, and the questions that He chooses not to answer are fine with me too.
Some things are best left that way.

I am learning to live, to be, to become.
I am done, finished with doing and proving.
It's just not for me.
It's just not for me!"

The Beginning

About the Author

Nevlynn L. Johnson is a consultant with In The Lead, an Atlanta based business. He currently consults with a national youth organization and several churches specializing in the development of outreach and youth programs. He also speaks and lectures on a variety of topics, such as at risk youth, race relations, and community development.

If you like this book or would like to request Nevlynn Johnson as a speaker or consultant, please contact him at www.nevjohnson.com or email him at nevlynn@nevjohnson.com. Please send your correspondence to:

> Attention: Faith, Courage, and Wisdom
> 3588 Highway 138 S.E., #193
> Stockbridge, GA 30281

0-595-16741-1